Shakespeare's Island

Shakespeare's Island

St. Helena and The Tempest

David J. Jeremiah

Copyright © 2015 David J. Jeremiah

All rights reserved.

ISBN-13: 9781514721735
ISBN-10: 1514721732

'A little traveling Stage-Troupe, is St. Helena really, all performance—A Plantation, sent out years since by its metropolitan Planet...'

THOMAS PYNCHON, *MASON & DIXON*, 1997

'The general told me about the island of St Helena, lying between the equator and the tropic. He said it was a very fertile country and almost completely uninhabited, a place moreover easy and convenient to fortify, and having constructed defences, to plant a colony...'

RICHARD MADOX, *DIARIUM OXON*, 1582

Table of Contents

Acknowledgements · ix
A Note to the Reader · · · · · · · · · · · · · · · · · · xi
Preface · xiii
Introduction · xv
Chapter 1 *Here is Everything Advantageous to Life* · · · · · · 1
Chapter 2 *The Tempest* · 23
Chapter 3 *The Great Globe Itself* · · · · · · · · · · · · · · · · · · 29
Chapter 4 *We Must Prepare to Meet with Caliban* · · · · · · 37
Chapter 5 *This Island's Mine* · 40
Chapter 6 *As You from Crimes Will Pardoned Be* · · · · · · · 47
Chapter 7 *Rapt in Secret Studies* · · · · · · · · · · · · · · · · · · · 50
Chapter 8 *When It Is Bak'd with Frost* · · · · · · · · · · · · · · 63
Chapter 9 *Had I Plantation of This Isle* · · · · · · · · · · · · · 71
Chapter 10 *Epilogue* · 85
Postscript: Ban', Ban', Ca-Caliban · · · · · · · · 87
Bibliography · 95
Notes · 101

Acknowledgements

A good library is essential when writing a book relying largely on historical and literary material. I have been fortunate in being able to use the British Library, assisted by its unfailingly helpful and courteous staff. Thousands of miles away, in the South Atlantic, I came across a less famous collection of books in the Jamestown Public Library in Saint Helena. The reference section there is home to a large number of books about the island, some of which are difficult to track down elsewhere. I have spent many an hour sifting through these, an experience made all the more enjoyable by the congenial staff and the historic surroundings. My debt to previous works is, I hope, fully acknowledged in the bibliography, references, and notes. But my greatest debt is to my wife, Joy. Without her encouragement and tactful persuasion to complete it, this book would never have existed.

A Note to the Reader

This book is published in the same format wherever it is available for purchase. This has made it necessary to choose between British and American spelling and grammar. I have chosen the first alternative – believing that American readers will readily understand that an Englishman writes in the style of his home country. Where British usage offers alternatives that coincide with standard American usage I have used those alternatives.

I have, throughout the book, quoted extensively from documents written in the sixteenth and early seventeenth centuries, and have not been entirely consistent in choosing between the use of original or modernized spelling. Original spelling brings with it a greater sense of the time in which it was written, but can be difficult for the general reader to follow. I have modernized long or difficult texts but retained the charm of the original where it is readily understandable. The inconsistency is most marked in extracts taken from the diary of Richard Madox. Madox wrote some of his diary in English, and other parts in Greek, Latin or cipher. Extracts from all but the first of these are, of necessity, given in modern English.

Preface

For about twenty-five years, I lived and worked on small islands: in the Pacific, the South Atlantic, the West Indies, and finally, in the case of Alderney, the English Channel. For a little over six of these years, I was the attorney general of Saint Helena. It was there I realized that the island – its physical characteristics and history – had resonances in one of Shakespeare's best loved plays.

The Tempest explores how people react differently to new experiences following their arrival on a small island. Some are changed as a result, some remain resolutely the same, and others seemingly find themselves possessed of a compulsion to address (positively, they would say) issues that only they can see the answers to. The characters in the play reflect this diversity: Alonso is changed (for the better), Antonio remains resolutely the same (irremediably evil), and Gonzalo wants to run the place. There are, in my experience, plenty of Gonzalos in the world. As a governor of Saint Helena once observed, somewhat ruefully, 'Saint Helena is a small island surrounded by an ocean of advice.'

The island is one of the remotest places on earth: the nearest land, other than a few rocks and islets off its own coast, is Ascension Island, over seven hundred miles to the north. The African coast is some twelve hundred miles away, and South America lies over two thousand miles to the west. Ask most people what they know about Saint Helena and they will mention Napoleon. But when asked for the island's location, a good number of these will tell you that it is in the Mediterranean, confusing it with Elba. Elba is where Napoleon was first exiled and from where he escaped in 1815. Following his defeat at Waterloo, he was sent to Saint Helena, from where there could be no escape. He died on the island in 1821. There are three places on the island associated with Napoleon: the Briars Pavilion, where he spent several weeks as a guest of the Balcombe family; Longwood House, his home (although he hardly regarded it as such); and his tomb, on the site that he chose himself. The tomb bears no inscription and is now empty; his body was moved to Les Invalides in Paris in 1840.

For over four hundred years, it has only been possible to travel to or from the island by sea; Napoleon arrived there on the HMS *Northumberland*. Apart from yachts and cruise vessels, Saint Helena's lifeline for many years has been the RMS *St Helena*. The 'RMS' signifies that it is a Royal Mail Ship: Saint Helena is a United Kingdom Overseas Territory and even has its own postcode, STHL 1ZZ, which suffices for the whole of the island. But as I write, Saint Helena is about to become less of an island; an airport is due to open there in 2016. This seems an apt time to publish this book.

Introduction

If there is such a thing as a national play, then England's is surely *The Tempest*. When London hosted the Olympic Games in 2012, lines from the play were used in both the opening and closing ceremonies. In the opening ceremony, Kenneth Branagh delivered Caliban's famous speech:

> Be not afeard. The isle is full of noises,
> Sounds and sweet airs that give delight and hurt not.
> Sometimes a thousand twangling instruments
> Will hum about mine ears; and sometimes voices,
> That if I then had waked after long sleep,
> Will make me sleep again; and then in dreaming,
> The clouds, methought, would open and show riches
> Ready to drop upon me, that when I waked
> I cried to dream again.
>
> (3.2.135–143)

This reached a global audience of millions. Danny Boyle, artistic director for the ceremony, explained his choice of Caliban to evoke a sense of national pride:

> The speech is about the wondrous beauty of the island and his deep, deep affection and devotion to it.[1]

A large part of this book is about Caliban and my attempt to identify the man who provided the inspiration for the character. It is also about the island for which that man had such deep affection and devotion.

There have been many candidates put forward for the island of *The Tempest*. (It is unnamed in the play.) These include Pantelleria, Lampedusa, Vulcano, Bermuda, and Corfu. Bermuda, the only suggested location generally agreed upon by scholars, was first proposed by Edmond Malone, the Irish-born Shakespearean scholar, in the early nineteenth century, when he came across what are generally referred to as the 'Bermuda Pamphlets' – which deal with a shipwreck in Bermuda in 1609. Malone remains a greatly respected authority on Shakespeare and any theory put forward by him carries considerable weight. With this in mind, we should not be surprised that Bermuda has remained, for most commentators on the play, the main contender, but the evidence for this does not amount to much more than a constant repetition of the idea. All the islands put forward over the years as the island of *The Tempest* lack a significant requirement – a Caliban. Saint Helena provides us with him and much more.

No real island will have all the attributes of Shakespeare's island. This would require one where moles are co-resident with marmosets and that was once home to a witch from Algiers who worshipped a Patagonian god. Clearly, there is no such place. We can only point to an island that has both a character – and an event entirely separate from that character – in its history that are demonstrably reflected in the play. An island that was once home to a man with remarkable similarities to Caliban – and offers us a singular episode in its past with a parallel in the play that can hardly be a coincidence – must be taken seriously as Shakespeare's inspiration for his island.

This is also a book about the creative process. Much has been written about what are generally termed 'Shakespeare's sources'. For some, this has been a lifetime's work, as with Geoffrey Bullough, whose *Narrative and Dramatic Sources of Shakespeare* extends over eight volumes. The main plots of Shakespeare's plays are mostly traceable to works written by others; but *The Tempest* is an exception to this, along with *Love's Labour's Lost* and *A Midsummer Night's Dream*.

Without a source for the play as a whole, we are left with only particular lines within *The Tempest* that can be traced back to their literary origins. For example:

> Ye elves of hills, brooks, standing lakes and groves,
> And ye that on the sands with printless foot
> Do chase the ebbing Neptune, and do fly him
> When he comes back; you demi-puppets that
> By moonshine do the green sour ringlets make,
> Whereof the ewe not bites; and you whose pastime
> Is to make midnight-mushrooms, that rejoice
> To hear the solemn curfew, by whose aid –
> Weak masters though ye be – I have bedimmed
> The noontide sun, called forth the mutinous winds,
> And 'twixt the green sea and the azured vault

> Set roaring war; to the dread-rattling thunder
> Have I given fire and rifted Jove's stout oak
> With his own bolt: the strong-based promontory
> Have I made shake, and by the spurs plucked up
> The pine and cedar; graves at my command
> Have waked their sleepers, ope'd and let 'em forth
> By my so potent art.
>
> (5.1.33–50)

This passage was derived from Medea's incantation in Ovid's *Metamorphoses*, probably as rendered in Arthur Golding's translation of 1567.

Throughout this book, I have noted a large number of lines in *The Tempest* that echo lines to be found elsewhere, and which also have a bearing on my main theme. These are of interest – but, as Charles Frey reminds us in his *The Tempest and the New World*, they must be treated with caution:

> We tend not to appreciate the extent to which some themes, situations, incidents and even phrases in *The Tempest* were part of the common coin of Shakespeare's day…We need to read the voyage literature, therefore, not necessarily to find out what Shakespeare read, but to ascertain what Shakespeare and his audience together would have been likely to know.[2]

What I believe – and have set out to prove – is that a real man who lived on Saint Helena in the sixteenth century was the prototype Caliban, and that an Elizabethan sea captain's plan for the island is, separately and clearly, used by Shakespeare as an important theme in *The Tempest*.

I

Here is Everything Advantageous to Life

Saint Helena was uninhabited and (as far as is known) previously unvisited by man when Admiral Juan de Nova came across it on 21 May, 1502. There could have been no doubt in the admiral's mind that the island was Portuguese – in accordance with the terms of the Treaty of Tordesillas. The treaty, entered into by Portugal and Spain in 1494, had resolved, at least between the parties, all questions of title to the newly discovered (and some yet to be discovered) parts of the globe. The meridian line drawn through both poles from a point some 370 leagues west of the Cape Verde Islands was to separate Portuguese claims from those of Spain: new lands east of the line would be Portuguese, and those west of it would be Spanish. Saint Helena is east of the line. In any event, although himself Spanish, the admiral was in the service of the king of Portugal and in command of the king's fleet. 21 May is the feast day of Saint Helena, the mother of the Emperor Constantine, and the island was named in her honour.

At least, this is accepted history. In fact, in the Western Church Calendar, which the Portuguese would, one would think, have been observing, Saint Helena's feast day falls on

18 August. To make matters still murkier, 21 May is the eve of the feast day of Saint Helen, Virgin of Auxerre.[3] But it has been suggested that any controversy over the identity of the saint whose name was given to the island can be resolved by reference to the Greek Orthodox Calendar. In this, the traditional date of the death of Constantine is 21 May, and his mother shares this feast day with him.[4]

An English account, by William Barret, written long after the event (in 1584), suggests that the island was 'discovered by a ship that came from the Indies in a great storm.'[5] 'Discovered' was a word used with some looseness at the time, and it is possible that Barret is referring to a visit later than de Nova's – he describes the Portuguese finding things on the island that only they could have introduced there. Barret was the English consul in Aleppo, the port of Tripoli in Syria, and did not visit Saint Helena; but, aside from his apparent error as to the circumstances of its initial discovery, he was remarkably well-informed – he writes, for example, that the island is sixteen degrees south of the equator (the correct co-ordinate is 15.9500° S).

The Portuguese did not colonize Saint Helena but made use of it as a safe anchorage and watering place. It became the practice of their fleets to gather there before completing the voyage back to Portugal from India.[6] Because of this, we may be reasonably certain that Ferdinand Magellan, the leader of the expedition that later achieved the first circumnavigation of the globe, was an early visitor. Magellan served as a soldier in India. He fought at the Battle of Diu in 1509, the engagement that established Portuguese control of the Indian Ocean, and he was present at the taking of Malacca in 1511. By 1512 he was back in Lisbon. Homeward bound, he had stopped at Saint Helena. From his ship at anchor in what is now James Bay, Magellan would have seen a rocky and mountainous island with a welcome stream of fresh water – today known as the Run – emptying into the sea. He might have been able to make out a small building on the shore. Legend has it that one of de Nova's ships was broken up at Saint Helena and its timbers used for the construction of a small chapel. If true, and assuming that the tradition of successively rebuilding churches on the same site was subsequently followed, this would make Saint James's Church, in Jamestown, Saint Helena, the second oldest Christian site south of the equator – and the oldest still used as a place of worship. (The Portuguese had built a chapel at Mossel Bay, South Africa, in 1501,[7] although no trace of this now remains.)

When Magellan went ashore – it is difficult to believe that he would not have – there were structures to be seen around the chapel, shelters for sailors left on the island to recover from scurvy. There would also have been some signs of cultivation, as there still are today along the course of the Run. But he did not come across anyone who called the island home – seamen who had recovered from scurvy would sail back to Portugal on the next available ship. The island's first long-term resident had yet to arrive.

The Portuguese tried to keep their discovery of the island, and its location, to themselves. This was in keeping with the established practice of the time. But cartography was coming of age, and, by the middle of the sixteenth century, Saint Helena had quite literally been put on the map. Pierre Desceliers, one of the Dieppe school of mapmakers who had access to both French and Portuguese sea-charts, showed it in his world map of 1550. The map is now in the British Library.

It is a manuscript prepared for a patron of high rank, probably either King Henri II of France or the Duc de Montmorency, both of whose coats of arms are depicted in it. It is not for the use of navigators – it is a work of art, a picture of the world, and it did not appear in print. It follows from this that Shakespeare did not see it. But we should bear in mind Charles Frey's wise reminder, referred to in my Introduction, to recognize what was the common coin of the time, the sorts of things that Shakespeare and his audience would have had a mutual awareness of – or believed themselves to know – about the recently discovered world. Desceliers' map depicts people as well as places. In central Africa, he shows a male figure with a square head set in his chest – complete with eyes. In *The Tempest*, Shakespeare refers to the following:

…such men
Whose heads stood in their breasts,…
(3.3.46/47)

For good measure, the map also shows images of dog-headed men: Caliban is referred to in *The Tempest* as a 'puppy-headed monster' (2.2.151/2).

If there was any lingering mystery in England about the whereabouts of Saint Helena it was swept away when the Flemish cartographer, Abraham Ortelius, published his 'World Map' in 1564, and followed this up with his famous collection of maps, *Theatrum Orbis Terrarum* (Theatre of the World), in 1570. Saint Helena, Ascension Island, and Tristan da Cunha were all featured and placed in their more or less correct positions by Ortelius.

An Englishman, Thomas Cavendish (also spelled 'Candish'), visited Saint Helena in 1588. The third circumnavigator of the world, Cavendish was heading for home, fame, and fortune. The account of his call at Saint Helena, in *The Prosperous Voyage of M. Thomas Candish esquire into the South sea, and so around about the circumference of the whole earth, begun in the yere 1586*, is as delightful as it is comprehensive, and it is about as good as travel writing in this (or any) period gets. It was also available to Shakespeare, having been printed in Richard Hakluyt's *Principall Navigations* in 1598, the same work from which he took his reference to the 'New Map' of *Twelfth Night*. It is the earliest eyewitness account of the island by an Englishman, and, because it was known to Shakespeare and, as importantly, others in England at the time he wrote *The Tempest*, I have set it out here at some length:

> The eighth day of June by break of day we fell in sight of the island of Saint Helena.
>
> The island is a very high land, and lieth in the main sea standing as it were in the middest of the sea between the mainland of Brazil and the coast of Guinea.
>
> The same day about two or three of the clock in the afternoon we went on shore, where we found a marvellous fair and pleasant valley, wherein divers handsome buildings and houses were set up, and especially one which was a church, which was tiled and whited on the outside very fair, and made with a porch, and within the church at the upper end was set an altar, whereon stood a very large table set in a frame having

in it the picture of Our Saviour Christ upon the Cross and the image of Our Lady praying, with divers other histories curiously painted. The sides of the Church were all hanged with stained clothes having many devices drawn in them.

There are two houses adjoining to the Church, which serve for kitchens to dress meat in, with necessary rooms and houses of office: the coverings of the said houses are made flat, whereon is planted a very fair vine, and through both the said houses runneth a very good and wholesome stream of fresh water.

There is also right over against the said church a fair causeway made up with stones reaching unto a valley by the seaside, in which valley is planted a garden, wherein grow a great store of pompions and melons: and upon the said causeway is a frame erected whereon hang two bells wherewith they ring to mass; and hard unto it is a cross set up, which is squared, framed and made very artificially of free stone, whereon is carved in ciphers what time it was builded, which was in the year of our Lorde 1571.

This valley is the fairest and largest low plot in all the island, and it is marvellous sweet and pleasant, and planted in every place either with fruit trees, or with herbs. There are fig trees, which bear fruit continually, and marvellous plentifully: for on every tree you shall have blossoms, green figs, and ripe figs, all at once: and it is so all the year long: the reason is that the island standeth so near the sun. There be also great store of lemon trees, orange trees, pomegranate trees, pomecitron trees, date trees, which bear fruit as the fig trees do, and are planted carefully and very artificially[8] with very pleasant walks under and between them, and the said walks be overshadowed with the leaves of the trees: and in every void[9] place is planted parsley, sorrel, basil, fennel, aniseed, mustard seed, radishes, and many special good herbs: and the fresh water brook runneth through divers places of this orchard, and may with very small pains be made to water any one tree in the valley.

This fresh water stream cometh from the tops of the mountains, and falleth from the cliff into the valley the height of a cable,[10] and hath many arms out of it, which refresh the whole island, and almost every tree in it. The island is altogether high mountains and steep valleys, and down below in some of the valleys, marvellous store of all these kinds of fruits before spoken of do grow: there is greater store of trees growing in the tops of the mountains than below in the valleys: but it is wonderful laboursome and also dangerous travelling up unto them and down again, by reason of the height and steepness of the hills.

There is also upon this island great store of partridges, which are very tame, not making any great haste to fly away though one come very near them, but only to run away, and get up into the steep cliffs: we killed some of them with a fowling piece. They differ very much from our partridges which are in England both in bigness and also in colour. For they be as big as an hen, and are of an ash colour, and live in coveys twelve, sixteen, and twenty together.

There are likewise no less store of pheasants in the island, which are also marvellous big and fat, surpassing those which are in our country in bigness and in numbers. They differ not very much in colour from the partridges before spoken of. We found moreover in this place great store of guinea-cocks, which we call turkeys, of colour black and white, with red heads: they are much about the same bigness which ours be of in England: their eggs be white, and as big as a turkey's egg.

There are in this island thousands of goats, which the Spaniards call cabritos, which are very wild: you shall see one or two hundred of them together, and sometimes you may behold them going in a flock almost a mile long. Some of them are as big as an ass with a mane like an horse and a beard hanging down to the very ground: they will climb up the cliffs which are so steep that a man would think it a thing impossible for any living thing to go there. We took and killed many of them for all their swiftness: for there are thousands of them upon the mountains.

Here are in like manner are great store of swine which be very wild and fat, and of marvellous bigness: they keep altogether upon the mountains, and will very seldom abide any man to come near them, except it be by mere chance when they be found asleep, or otherwise, according to their kind, be taken in the mire.

We found in the houses at our coming three slaves which were negroes, and one which was born in the island of Java, which told us that the East Indian fleet, which were in number five sails, the least whereof were in burthen eight or nine hundred tons, all laden with spices and Calicut cloth, with store of treasure and very rich stones and pearls, were gone from the said island of Saint Helena but twenty days before we came thither.

This island hath been found of a long time by the Portuguese, and hath been altogether planted by them, for their refreshing as they come from the East Indies. By reason of these things they suffer none to inhabit there that might spend up the fruit of the island, except some very few sick persons in their company, which they stand in doubt will not live until they come home, whom they leave there to refresh themselves, and take away the year following, if they live so long. They touch here rather in their coming home from the East Indies than at their going thither, because they are thoroughly furnished with corn when they set out of Portugal, but are meanly victualled at their coming from the Indies, where there groweth little corn.

The twentieth day of June having taken in wood and water and refreshed ourselves with such things as we found there, and making clean our ship, we set sail about eight of the clock in the night toward England. At our setting sail we had the wind at south-east, and we hauled away north-west and by west. The wind is commonly off the shore at this island of Saint Helena.[11]

It is a seaman's narrative; we have details of the anchorage, the island is given a well-plotted position, and we learn of the prevailing wind, an important detail in the age of sail. But it is also a businessman's account, almost an inventory. The attributes of the island are catalogued: it is a 'very high land', a settlement of sorts has been established, and there is fresh water and an abundance of food. Very little in the way of husbandry is required; goats, pigs, pheasants, and partridges have been introduced and have flourished. But there is more than a hint of disappointment – although not in the qualities of the island. Cavendish had missed the Portuguese fleet by twenty days, 'all laden with spices and Calicut cloth, with store of treasure and very rich stones and pearls'. This was the man who, some seven months earlier off the coast of California, had taken the Spanish galleon the *Santa Ana*. Had he also taken a Portuguese vessel at Saint Helena he would have ranked with Drake among Elizabethan privateers.

Cavendish arrived back in England too late to face the Armada – he missed it by a few weeks – but he had found his place in history. He had also ensured that the existence, attributes, and whereabouts of Saint Helena would soon become firmly fixed in the English mind: Richard Hakluyt was to take care of this. On 17 November 1589, spurred on by Cavendish's achievement, Hakluyt signed off his landmark book, *Principall Navigations, Voyages and Discoveries of the English Nation*: 'Whereunto is added the last most renowned English navigation round the whole Globe of the Earth'. Cavendish's call at Saint Helena was of sufficient importance to warrant a special mention in Hakluyt's *'Epistle Dedicatorie'* – prefacing the *Principall Navigations*:

> For, which of the kings of this land before her Majesty, had their banners ever seen in the Caspian

Sea? Who ever found English Consuls and agents at Tripoli in Syria, and which is more, who ever heard of Englishmen at Goa before now? What English ships did heretofore ever anchor in the mighty river of Plate? Pass and re-pass the impassable (in former opinion) strait of Magellan, range along the coast of Chile, Peru, and all the backside of Nova Hispania, further than any Christian ever passed, traverse the mighty breadth of the South sea, double the famous Cape of Bona Speranza,[12] arrive at the isle of Saint Helena, and last of all return home most richly laden with the commodities of China, as the subjects of this now flourishing monarchy have done?[13]

A Dutchman, Jan Huygen van Linschoten, visited the island in 1589, eleven months after Cavendish, and published a description of it in 1596. An English version of this appeared in 1598, *Iohn Huighen van Linschoten his Discours of Voyages into ye Easte & West Indies*. It gives us much the same picture as that conveyed by the account of Cavendish's visit; an island of plenty where fresh water and food are there for the taking:

> When the Portuguese first discovered it, there were not any beasts, nor fruit, at all within the island, but only great store of fresh water, which is excellent good, and falleth down from the mountains, and so runneth in great abundance into the valley, where the church standeth, and from then by small channels, into the sea, where the Portuguese fill their vessels full of fresh water, and wash their clothes: so that it is a great benefit for them, and a pleasant sight to behold, how clear

and in how many streams the water runneth down into the valley, which may be thought a miracle, considering the dryness of the country together with the stony rocks and hills therein. The Portuguese have by little and little brought many beasts into it, and in the valleys planted all sorts of fruits: which have grown there in so great abundance, that it is almost incredible...It seemeth to be an earthly Paradise.[14]

Linschoten's 1598 edition was illustrated and a plate entitled Insula D. Helenae provides a readily recognizable depiction of the island, rising almost sheer from the sea. There is some artistic licence, but it is less than a person who has not seen the island might think. It offers an odd combination, awesome yet welcoming. It is easy to understand Linschoten's description of the mood on board when the island was sighted, 'Whereat there was such great joy in the ship, as if we had been in heaven.' There is a colour print in the museum in Jamestown, dated 1589 and attributed to Linschoten. It shows the chapel, buttressed by a building on either side. The Run, as viewed from the sea, flows down the left side of the valley; either this is an error or it has substantially changed its course over the years. What is now known as the Heart Shaped Waterfall (described by Cavendish as falling 'from the cliff into the valley the height of a cable') is depicted as a deep 'V' in the landscape and is correctly placed inland – although, in fact, it is not visible from the sea. The valley is fertile, and there is good hunting in the hills. The message is clear: this is an island of plenty, providing all that a fleet requires. A Portuguese fleet, consisting of six vessels (all named), is in the foreground.

In 1593, two English vessels, the *Penelope* and the *Edward Bonaventure*, visited Saint Helena. The latter vessel had seen action against the Armada under its captain, James Lancaster. A strange sight awaited Lancaster and his crew on the island – as recounted by Edmund Barker, Lancaster's lieutenant:

> I found an Englishman, one John Segar of Bury in Suffolk, who was left there eighteen months before by Abraham Kendall, who put in there with the *Royal Merchant*, and left him there to refresh him on the island, being otherwise likely to have perished on board ship; and at our coming we found him as fresh in colour and in as good plight of body to our seeming as might be, but crazed in mind and half out of his wits, as afterward we perceived; for whether he were put in fright of us, not knowing at first what we were, whether friends or foes, or of sudden joy when he understood we were his old consorts and countrymen, he became idle-headed, and for eight days space neither night nor day took any natural rest, and so at length died for lack of sleep.[15]

According to another account:

> We found of his [Segar's] drying some forty goats. The party made him, for want of apparel, two suits of goat skins with the hairy side outwards, like unto the savages of Canada.[16]

This is the footnote in history of John Segar, of Bury Saint Edmunds, Suffolk. Here we have animal skins made into clothing for a man found alone on a remote island – as 'savages' might wear. Segar is not Caliban, but there is the beginning of an idea here. The scholar Edmond Malone, without saying how he knew this, claimed in 1821 that Caliban's costume in early productions was an animal skin, as 'originally prescribed by the poet himself.'[17]

Whatever the truth of William Barret's account of the circumstances of the island's discovery by the Portuguese, in a 'great storm' – which, as we have seen, might not be reliable – Saint Helena did later establish itself as a place to seek respite from the most challenging of conditions at sea. In 1603, two ships of the recently formed East India Company, the *Dragon*[18] and the *Hector*, encountered bad weather off the Cape of Good Hope in the course of which the *Dragon* lost her rudder:

> This struck a present fear into the hearts of all men; so that the best of us and most experienced knew not what to do. And specially seeing ourselves in such a tempestuous sea and so stormy a place, so that I think there be few worse in all the world. Now our ship drove up and down in the sea like a wreck…Our case was miserable and very desperate.[19]

Gonzalo, in *The Tempest*, comes to mind. Speculating that the boatswain has 'no drowning mark upon him'[20] – and reflecting the proverb of the time that a man who is born to be hanged will not drown – Gonzalo gives us the following:

> If he be not born to
> be hanged, our case is miserable.
>
> (1.1.32–33)

'Our case was miserable' and 'Our case is miserable' are too strikingly similar to ignore. Shakespeare did not hesitate to borrow lines that he liked, often many years after he had first come across them.

Lancaster's voyage was what we would now describe as high profile – and a number of accounts of it appeared in London. When things had seemed close to hopeless in the South Atlantic (the storm-tossed ships were out of sight of land for three months), Lancaster famously wrote to his employers, the East India Company: 'I live at the devotion of the winds and seas.'[21] The letter was passed to the captain of the *Hector*, with instructions to head for England and abandon the *Dragon* to its fate. The following day the *Hector* was still within sight, its captain having defied Lancaster's orders – his commission – to leave the *Dragon*. On seeing this, Lancaster uttered his equally famous words: 'These men regard no commission.'[22] Unlike in the rigid society of contemporary England, men made their own decisions at sea. This is reflected in the opening scene of *The Tempest*, where Alonso, King of Naples, tries to give instructions to the boatswain, who responds, 'What cares these roarers[23] for the name of king?'[24]

The decision of the captain of the *Hector*, Alexander Cole, to stay with the *Dragon* was vindicated a few days later when the weather improved and further efforts could be made to render the *Dragon* capable of continuing its voyage. With the help of the *Hector*'s crew, a makeshift rudder was fitted to the *Dragon* and the two ships reached Saint Helena on the morning of 16 June: 'at the sight whereof there was no small rejoicing among us.'

The *Dragon* and the *Hector* arrived back in England on 11 September 1603, and the men who had been on board resumed, at least for the time being, the normality of life on shore. We may reasonably assume that at least some of those who sailed on these ships visited the theatre when in London, and it is known that two of Shakespeare's plays were later acted on board the *Dragon*. The following are extracts from the journal of William Keeling, the *Dragon*'s captain, in 1607:

> September 5, 1607. I sent the Portuguese interpreter according to his desire, aboard the Hector where he broke fast, and after came aboard me, where we had the Tragedy of Hamlet; and in the afternoon we went all together ashore, to see if we could shoot an elephant.
>
> September 29, 1607. Captain Hawkins dined with me, when my company acted King Richard the Second.
>
> March 31, 1608. I invited Captain Hawkins to a fish dinner, and had Hamlet acted aboard me: which I permit to keep my people from idleness and unlawful games, or sleep.[25]

These are not the only instances of plays staged on board vessels of the East India Company. In 1610, the captain of the *Peppercorn*, Nicholas Downton, wrote: 'My general invited me to dinner and to [a] play.'[26] There is nothing surprising about this; there was a long tradition of setting off to sea with the resources necessary to put on entertainments, as we are informed concerning Sir Humphrey Gilbert's preparations for a voyage to Newfoundland in 1583:

> For the solace of our people and allurement of the savages we were provided of music in good variety; not omitting the least toys as morris dancers, hobby horses, and May-like conceits to delight the savage people, whom we intended to win by all fair means possible.[27]

It was not just a matter of surviving shipwreck and scurvy; men took their culture with them when they sailed to foreign lands, and they enriched it when they returned home with accounts of their experiences. Shakespeare rubbed shoulders with such men. These included Thomas Lodge, a poet and fellow playwright. That Lodge was an influence on Shakespeare is beyond dispute. His prose romance *Rosalynde* was adapted for the stage by Shakespeare and became *As You Like It*. Shakespeare took the plot for the play, and a number of the names of the characters, from Lodge's work. Lodge claimed that he wrote *Rosalynde* while he was at sea, probably during a voyage to the Canaries, but this was not the end of his sea adventures. In 1592, he signed up to accompany Cavendish on what proved to be Cavendish's last voyage. During this, Lodge wrote, or at least commenced writing, his *Margarite of America*:

> Touching the place where I wrote this, it was in those straits christened by Magelan; in which place to the southward many wondrous Isles, many strange fishes, many monstrous Patagones withdrew my senses.[28]

17

We may pause to consider that the island of *The Tempest* contained a 'strange fish' in the shape of Caliban:

> What have we here, a man or a fish? Dead or alive?
> A fish: he smells like a fish, a very ancient and fish-like smell, a kind of not of the newest poor-John. A strange fish!
>
> (2.2.24–27)

Shakespeare clearly liked the idea. Alonso, speaking of his apparently lost son Ferdinand, has the lines:

> O thou mine heir
> Of Naples and Milan, what strange fish
> Hath made his meal on thee?
>
> (2.1.12–14)

Shakespeare's familiarity with *A Margarite of America*, as with *Rosalynde*, is most obvious in *As You Like It*. He came across Lodge's line, 'Plutarch saith that life is a stage play,'[29] and then gave us Jacque's famous speech:

> All the world's a stage,
> And all the men and women merely players.
> They have their exits and their entrances,
> And one man in his time plays many parts.
>
> (2.7.139–142)

Jacques continues the speech with the almost equally well-known lines about the seven ages of man – Lodge having provided Shakespeare with a poem on the same theme in *A*

Margarite of America, in which he describes how we pass from 'childish crying' to when 'mortall life on sodaine vanisheth.'[30]

We may be reasonably certain that Shakespeare knew Lodge personally; London was a small world, and Lodge was a noted playwright. Francis Meres, in his *Wit's Treasury*, published in 1598, tells us that Shakespeare was 'most excellent' for both comedy and tragedy and that Lodge was among 'the best' for comedy. But when Lodge put quill to paper in the South Atlantic, there was little room for comedy.

Attempts by Cavendish to get through to the Pacific were defeated by the elements, and the fleet, or what remained of it, fell back to the east coast of South America. Cavendish resolved to head for Saint Helena. He had, after all, experienced its advantages to a ship starved of supplies and with a crew seeking renewal of themselves after the privations of a difficult voyage:

> I showed them that I would beat for Saint Helena and there either make ourselves happy by mending or ending. This course in truth pleased none of them.[31]

Cavendish's command had become increasingly fragile and his men were right to doubt his decision; the attempt to 'beat for Saint Helena' proved futile. The winds and currents are such that Saint Helena is not easily reached under sail from South America, and Cavendish was unable to repeat his earlier success in landing there: 'It was not God's will so great a blessing should befall me.'[32]

We do not know if Lodge was with Cavendish at this point in the voyage. Lodge could have been on either the *Roebuck* or Cavendish's *Galleon Leicester*, each of which is next recorded as being in harbour in England on the same date, although they may well have arrived there separately – we have no date or dates showing when either of them first reached England. If Lodge was on the *Galleon Leicester* as it neared Saint Helena (the *Roebuck* was not with the *Galleon Leicester* at this point), then he was with Cavendish and may at least have glimpsed the island. Certainly, by then, he would have heard a great deal about it from Cavendish.

Saint Helena, which rises to a height of two thousand six hundred and ninety-seven feet,[33] may be seen from a considerable distance from a ship at sea. The entry relating to Cavendish in the *Dictionary of National Biography*, citing an account by M. J. Jane,[34] suggests that Cavendish 'got within two leagues' of the island – from where it would have been clearly visible.[35] Samuel Purchas, writing in 1625, in *Purchas His Pilgrimes*, and ostensibly relying on Cavendish's account, states that he got within eighteen leagues of it, from where it might have been seen in favourable conditions. But this seems to have been an error of transcription; according to Cavendish, the distance was eighty leagues, not eighteen. This would have put the island out of sight. Certainly, there was no landfall at Saint Helena and Cavendish does not record a sighting of the island.

Having failed to make Saint Helena, Cavendish tried to reach Ascension Island, where, under normal circumstances, vessels did not call. (Lancaster's *Dragon* was to simply pass by within sight of it in 1603 – 'No ships touch at this island, for it is altogether barren and without water.'[36]) But Cavendish had descended into despair and his need was not for water:

> My spirit was clean spent wishing myself upon any desert place in the world there to die.[37]

Gonzalo, in *The Tempest*, again comes to mind:

> Now would I give a thousand furlongs of sea
> for an acre of barren ground – long heath, brown furze,
> anything. The wills above be done, but I would fain die
> a dry death.
>
> (1.1.64–67)

Could Shakespeare have seen Cavendish's account?

In his instructions to his executor, Tristram Gorges, Cavendish required that his letter be delivered 'only' to Sir George Carey.[38] Carey was the son of Lord Hunsdon, the lord chamberlain, under whose patronage Shakespeare's company then performed; the company was known as the Lord Chamberlain's Men. Such support was important; the law required players to be attached to a baron 'or to any other honourable personage of greater degree.' Failing to have a patron subjected players to criminal penalties. To an actor and writer of plays, it did not come any better than to be one of the Lord Chamberlain's Men – it was the lord chamberlain who was in charge of putting on dramatic entertainments at court.

Sir George was as enthusiastic as his father in patronizing the players, perhaps more so. When the old man died, the company briefly became Lord Hunsdon's Men under the patronage of his son, who had inherited the title. A few months later, when the new Lord Hunsdon became lord chamberlain, the company resumed its status as the Lord Chamberlain's Men.

Taking over as the players' patron was not simply a token gesture on Carey's part; he liked his entertainment, and we have a record of him putting on a play for the queen following dinner at his home in the Blackfriars in 1601:

> The Queen dined this day privately at my Lord Chamberlain's; I came even now from the Blackfriars, where I saw her at the play with all her *candidae auditrices*.[39]

Carey also nurtured talent. Robert Johnson, who later wrote music for *The Tempest* – Ariel's songs *Full fathom five* and *Where the bee sucks* – was indentured to Carey for around seven years, commencing on 29 March 1596. Johnson was a relative of Emilia Lanier, considered by some to be the 'Dark Lady' of Shakespeare's sonnets. Shakespeare and Emilia certainly knew each other. Emilia, born Emilia Bassano, was the illegitimate daughter of Baptist Bassano, a court musician. She later became the mistress of the first Lord Hunsdon, Carey's father. When she became pregnant by Hunsdon, Emilia was married off to Alphonse Lanier – like Johnson, a musician. It was probably Emilia's influence that enabled Johnson to acquire his position with Sir George.

Carey was less supportive, however, when Shakespeare's company sought to establish itself in a public theatre at the Blackfriars: he is listed among the objectors to the project, which was delayed until after his death. It seems that he liked the entertainment provided by plays but not the prospect of nuisance created by throngs of theatregoers in his otherwise quiet neighbourhood. But his contribution to drama was to live on: through Johnson's music in *The Tempest*, and, perhaps, from papers in his possession that came to the attention of Shakespeare.

II

The Tempest

The first recorded performance of *The Tempest* was on 'Hallomas nyght' (1 November) 1611.[40] Shakespeare's company was by then the King's Men, and this was an entertainment put on for James I at court. It is generally considered to be the last play wholly written by Shakespeare, and it relies for much of its effect on a contemporary audience's knowledge of the world in which it was living. Ben Jonson said that Shakespeare 'was not of an age, but for all time'[41] – but Shakespeare did not write for us; we live in a very different world. One of our losses is that we cannot now experience *The Tempest* as it would have been experienced, and was intended to be experienced, by an audience of Shakespeare's time: an audience that lived in or visited what was then the busiest seaport in the world, an audience that would have included men who had been to sea and seen distant lands, an audience that needed to be persuaded that the playwright knew about such things. Rudyard Kipling was not writing entirely tongue in cheek when he suggested in a letter to *The Spectator* in 1916 that Shakespeare wrote *The Tempest* following an encounter with a drunken sailor at the Globe. Kipling knew, better than most of us, about the diverse sources of inspiration for creative writing.

We do not know whether Shakespeare had any personal experience of seafaring (or even that he ever saw the sea). As an actor, however, he was at least likely to have voyaged up the English coast to such places as Maldon and Ipswich, the sea route offering a better journey than the roads of the time. Even without such experience, as a writer he could conjure up such things in his imagination; and, in the unlikely event that this failed him, travellers' tales abounded. He shared with his audience a knowledge of what was topical. When, in *Twelfth Night*, Maria says of Andrew Aguecheek, 'He does smile his face into more lines than is in the new map with the augmentation of the Indies' (3.2.78–80), the reference is to Emery Molyneux's map of the world – published in 1599 in Richard Hakluyt's *Principall Navigations*.[42] The map shows a web of rhumb lines (a rhumb line is the line theoretically taken by a ship sailing on a constant compass bearing) and was the first to depict the whole of the East Indies, which were accordingly 'augmented'. A person without this knowledge misses the point (and wit) of what Maria is saying. Shakespeare clearly knew Hakluyt's work, and his borrowings from Hakluyt are probably more extensive than has been appreciated by most critics of his plays.[43] Shakespeare turned to Hakluyt in *Macbeth*, for example, in which Shakespeare gives us the line: 'Her husband's to Aleppo gone, master o'th'Tiger' (1.3.6.).[44] Hakluyt had written of a ship called the *Tiger*, destined for Aleppo, the port of Tripoli, in Syria.[45] Shakespeare also referred to the *Tiger*, or at least a ship of that name, in *Twelfth Night* – 'And this is he that did the Tiger board' (5.1.56).

Shakespeare read widely in the available accounts of the voyages of discovery, but much of what he derived from this is lost on us. *The Tempest*, for all its continued power as a play, contains a great deal that will mean little to a modern audience. Against this background, we may reasonably wish to know something of the real people, places, and events that Shakespeare had in mind when he wrote the play.

As we have seen, it is widely believed that *The Tempest* was inspired by a shipwreck at Bermuda in 1609. In the summer of that year, Sir George Summers (a Dorset man and former mayor of Lyme Regis) departed London in command of a fleet sailing for Virginia. A storm separated his ship, the *Sea Venture*, from the rest of the fleet, and it developed a massive leak, with water showing several feet above its ballast. When all seemed lost, the vessel was driven onto rocks off Bermuda and sank. Fortunately, all on board were saved. The crew constructed two small vessels from a combination of salvaged materials and local cedar, and the voyage was resumed, reaching Virginia in May 1610. Pamphlets published in London toward the end of 1610 recounted these events: an official report of the Virginia Company, *A True Declaration of the Estate of the Colonie in Virginia* (which contained a reference to 'this tragicall Comaedie', perhaps suggesting material for a play), and *A Discovery of the Barmudas* by Sylvester Jourdain, another Lyme Regis man. But neither of these accounts has much to offer as a source for *The Tempest*, and it is William Strachey's letter from Virginia, *A True Reportory of the Wracke*, dated 15 June 1610, that is generally considered to have been used by Shakespeare, although there is no evidence that it was published during his lifetime. The letter first appeared in print (in *Purchas His Pilgrimes*) in 1625, which is not to say that Shakespeare may not have seen it in manuscript, as those who assert its relevance maintain. But the only evidence of this is the theory itself, and it suffers the difficulty that the Virginia Company actively sought to suppress the letter, which was critical of its project. It is possible, however, even likely, that Shakespeare met Strachey (himself a poet of some stature) when Strachey arrived back in London in 1611, a matter of weeks before the first known performance of *The Tempest*. It is interesting to note that Strachey was a shareholder in the theatre at the Blackfriars in 1606.[46] He mixed with playwrights, and contributed a poem to the 1604 publication of Ben Jonson's *Sejanus His Fall*, the first performance of which was by Shakespeare's company at the Globe in 1603.

Some have gone so far as to say that events in Bermuda, including those reported by Strachey, were not just an influence on what Shakespeare wrote (that much may reasonably be accepted) but that Bermuda *is* the island of *The Tempest*. This ignores a great deal, not least that Bermuda is a group of islands, as Shakespeare would have been aware had he seen Strachey's letter – 'We found it to be the dangerous and dreaded island, or rather islands of the Bermuda.'[47] Shakespeare, in his sole reference to Bermuda in the play, describes it in the plural: 'the still-vext Bermoothes' (1.2.229). Equally inconvenient to the theory is that in the play Prospero has Ariel travel *from* the island *to* the Bermuda islands to fetch dew 'at midnight' (1.2.228). In short, Shakespeare tells us that Bermuda is not the island of the play.

The shipwreck at Bermuda may have been topical, but Shakespeare had been down this route before. When in *The*

Tempest he wrote 'room enough' (1.1.8), he echoed the 'sea-room' of *Pericles* (3.1.45). In *The Tempest* we have 'You do assist the storm' (1.1.14); and, in *Pericles*, 'Patience, good sir; do not assist the storm' (3.1.19). Add to this 'Blow till thou burst thy wind' (1.1.7) in *The Tempest* and 'Blow and split thyself' (3.1.44) in *Pericles* and it is difficult to conclude that Strachey's letter, or anything else written and circulated at the time about the Bermuda shipwreck, provided him with much material for his depiction of the storm in *The Tempest*. *Pericles* was in existence by 1608 and in print by 1609. The opening scene of *The Tempest* was so lacking in anything new to say about storms that Ben Jonson mocked it in his prologue to *Every Man In His Humour*, in which he promised that there would be no:

…rolled bullet heard
To say it thunders; nor tempestuous drum
Rumbles, to tell you when the storm doth come.[48]

The opening stage direction of *The Tempest* requires 'A tempestuous noise of thunder and lightning heard', and it is evident from Jonson's later reference in *Every Man in His Humour* to Caliban as a 'servant monster' that he has *The Tempest* in mind. The 'bullet' was a cannonball rolled over boards to replicate the sound of thunder, a device that Jonson clearly regarded as having had its day.

But we do learn more about the storm as the action of the play unfolds. Prospero has conjured it up through the agency of Ariel. Finishing his account of his labours, Ariel informs Prospero that the ship is safely in harbour, with the mariners in an enchanted sleep. The others who had been on board have been 'dispersed' by him about the island (1.2.220). The remaining ships of the fleet:

> ...are upon the Mediterranean flote
> Bound sadly home for Naples,
> Supposing that they saw the King's ship wracked
> And his great person perish.
> (1.2.234–237)

That Shakespeare places the island in the Mediterranean (necessarily for the plot) is of no consequence to any theory about the source of his inspiration for the island. Italianate backgrounds were conventional in plays of the period. Shakespeare derived his island more from the voyages of discovery in the Atlantic (and beyond) than from its ostensible setting, and it has been aptly described as 'a fragment of Italy transposed into the New World for a day or two.'[49] Shakespeare even gives us an ironic look back at the Old World from the island. Referring to the Italians cast up on the island, Miranda exclaims :

> O brave new world
> That has such people in't!
> (5.1.183–184)

Prospero responds that it is 'new to thee' (5.1.184).

But it is the brave new world so recently discovered by Europeans that the audience is intended to have in mind.

III

The Great Globe Itself

When, in *A Midsummer Night's Dream*, Puck says that he will 'put a girdle about the earth'[50] Shakespeare's audience was aware that this was a feat already achieved by voyagers – a little over forty years before Shakespeare's birth. It is difficult for us to appreciate how much the world expanded in the English consciousness as a result of this, hence the impact of Puck's claim that he will circle the globe in just forty minutes.[51] Shakespeare took a considerable interest in the voyages of discovery, knowing that references to them would resonate with his audience. Accounts of the first circumnavigation are an accepted source of *The Tempest*, and they are the best starting point when looking for the island of the play.

Ferdinand Magellan, the leader of the expedition that became the earliest voyage around the globe, was born in Portugal around 1480. As we have seen, he was an early visitor to Saint Helena. Following his return to Portugal, some years before the famous circumnavigation, he saw service in Morocco, where he was wounded; he walked with a limp for the rest of his life. He twice petitioned King Manuel for recognition of his services, but the king simply gave him the freedom to offer his skills elsewhere.

In 1517, Magellan left to try his luck in Spain, travelling via Seville to the court of King Charles I at Valladolid. It was there that he put a proposition to the Spanish king. Assisted by his friend Rui Faleiro, an astronomer, geographer, and astrologer, he would demonstrate, he claimed, that the source of the lucrative trade in spices, which the Portuguese had at that stage cornered for themselves, was, by virtue of the provisions of the Treaty of Tordesillas, to be found in Spanish territory. Faleiro was an important player in the project: he believed that he had solved the problem of establishing longitude while at sea. According to him, the Spice Islands fell to the east of 134 degrees longitude, which was the Asian extension of the meridian separating Portuguese and Spanish territorial claims under the treaty. But to take practical advantage of this there needed to be a route to the islands through Spanish waters. This was where Magellan came in. He had been to India and back via the Cape of Good Hope and Saint Helena. If the king backed the venture, he would sail west, avoiding lands and seas given to Portugal under the Treaty of Tordesillas, discover a strait through the inconveniently situated (but already discovered) South American continent, and sail on to the islands from where the spices came. These were the Moluccas in what is now Indonesia. The voyage would show the Moluccas to be on the Spanish side of the meridian. Charles liked the idea, and he approved the project.

A fleet was assembled, consisting of the *Trinidad, San Antonio, Concepcion, Victoria,* and *Santiago.* It left the Spanish port of San Lucar de Barrameda on 20 September 1519, but

Faleiro was not with it. In his *The Story of Magellan: And the Discovery of the Phillipines,* Hezekiah Butterworth wrote:

> The popular legend about this unhappy man was, that being an astrologer he had cast his own horoscope, and found that the expedition that he hoped to command would be lost, and so feigned madness.[52]

The casting of a horoscope was customary before embarking on a dangerous venture. As those who set off on this voyage were to amply demonstrate, there was a high likelihood that Faleiro would not have survived the experience; most of the participants, including Magellan, were not destined to return. Faleiro, whether through madness or not, seems to have made the right decision. The risks associated with such an enterprise are reflected in Shakespeare's reference in *The Tempest* to: 'Each putter-out of five for one' (3.3.48). This was a form of insurance – a voyager who returned safely would receive five times the amount deposited with a stakeholder prior to his departure.[53] The odds were significantly in favour of the insurer.

Accompanying Magellan on his flagship, the *Trinidad*, was Antonio Pigafetta, a Venetian citizen. It would seem that he had cast or commissioned a more auspicious horoscope than Faleiro's, as he was to be one of the few survivors of the enterprise. He also became the principal chronicler of the voyage. Shakespeare was clearly familiar with Pigafetta's account, which was first published in Italian and French, although an English translation, if he needed one,[54] was available to him in Richard Eden's *History of Travel*, which had been published in London in 1577. I have relied primarily on R. A. Skelton's translation of *Navigation and discovery of Upper India and the Isles of Molucca, where the cloves grow*, the manuscript of which is held in the Beinecke Rare Book and Manuscript Library of Yale University. As Skelton comments concerning information about the voyage: '...in one form or another – by oral, written or printed report – a good deal of it was diffused through other countries.'[55]

Magellan's fleet left Spain on 20 September 1519, from the port of San Lucar de Barrameda, and sailed south via Tenerife, which it reached by late September. It was subsequently becalmed off the coast of Guinea and then endured storms before reaching the equator:

> During these storms the body of St Anselm appeared to us several times. And among others on a night which was very dark, at a time of bad weather, the said saint appeared in the form of a lighted torch at the height of the maintop, and remained there more than two hours and a half, to the comfort of us all. For we were in tears, expecting only the hour of death, and when this holy light was about to leave us, it was so bright to the eyes of all that we were for more than quarter of an hour as blind as men calling for mercy. For without any doubt no man thought he would escape from that storm. Be it noted that, whenever this fire which represents the said St Anselm appears and descends on a ship (which is in a storm at sea), the ship never perishes.[56]

This is a description of Saint Elmo's fire, a natural phenomenon reported in many accounts of the voyages of the period, including Strachey's letter concerning the Bermuda shipwreck. It is as good a description of the phenomenon as any for Shakespeare to have drawn on for Ariel's efforts in *The Tempest*:

> I boarded the King's ship. Now on the beak,
> Now in the waist, the deck, in every cabin,
> I flamed amazement. Sometimes I'd divide
> And burn in many places; on the topmast;
> The yards, and bore sprit would I flame distinctly,
> Then meet and join.
>
> (1.2.196–201)

Ariel gives a display in three places: on the topmast, the yards, and 'bore sprit'. Pigafetta was to report the phenomenon a second time during his voyage, including on this occasion, the appearance of three saints:

> In this place we ran the very great risk of perishing. But the three bodies of St Anselm, St Nicholas and St Clare appeared to us, and forthwith the storm ceased.[57]

These extracts from Pigafetta provide the two things that are essential to what Shakespeare wrote in *The Tempest*: the three-part division of the spectacle that 'flamed amazement' and the subsequent safe delivery of a ship from the storm.

Pigafetta's account also includes a further event that is echoed in *The Tempest*. When the fleet reached South America

> One of the ships called the Santiago going to discover the coast was lost. But all the men were saved by a miracle, for they were not even wetted.[58]

To survive shipwreck is one thing, but to achieve this without getting wet is something out of the ordinary. In *The Tempest*, Gonzalo describes the survival of himself and others in Alonso's party:

> But for the miracle,
> I mean our preservation, few in millions
> Can speak like us.
> (2.1.6–8)

But what is truly miraculous, as in Pigafetta's account, is that they have been delivered from what was seemingly a shipwreck with their clothing unaffected:

> …the rarity of it is, which is indeed almost beyond credit –
> …That our garments being, as they were, drenched in the sea, hold notwithstanding their freshness and gloss, being rather new-dyed than stained with salt water.
> (2.1.60–66)

Shakespeare clearly liked this idea. Earlier in the play, he has Ariel tell Prospero the following:

> Not a hair perished;
> On their sustaining garments not a blemish,
> But fresher than before;
> (1.2.217–219)

In South America, the voyagers encountered the Tehuelche people. Based on reports such as Pigafetta's, these people were to enter the popular imagination of the time as giants, although there would have been some cynics back at home. Pigafetta described one of the 'giants' as 'so tall that the tallest of us only came up to his waist.'[59] This is in itself no more of a source for *The Tempest* than any number of similar accounts of strange things in strange places, but it does enable us to appreciate the irony in Antonio's lines:

> Travellers ne'er did lie,
> Though fools at home condemn 'em.
>
> (3.3.26)

South America, however, does provide us with one undeniable link with *The Tempest*. Magellan tricked two of the 'giants' into being fettered so that he could carry them away with him on the *Trinidad*:

> And when they saw the bolt across the fetters being struck with a hammer so as to rivet it and prevent them being opened, these giants were afraid. But the captain made signs to them that they should suspect nothing. Nevertheless, perceiving the trick that had been played on them, they began to blow and foam at the mouth like bulls, loudly calling on Setebos (that is the great devil) to help them.[60]

Shakespeare had such incidents in mind when he wrote:

> If I can recover him, and keep him tame, and get to Naples with him, he's a present for any emperor that ever trod on neat's leather.
>
> (2.2.70–73)

More importantly, the description of the capture of the two men tells us where Shakespeare came across Setebos, who is twice referred to in *The Tempest*.

When Caliban finds himself as helpless against Prospero as the giants had been against Magellan, he says:

> I must obey: his Art is of such pow'r,
> It would control my dam's god, Setebos,
> And make a vassal of him.
>
> (1.2.374–376)

Later in the play, when Ariel brings Caliban and his fellow conspirators before Prospero, there is further mention of Setebos:

> O Setebos, these be brave spirits indeed!
> How fine my master is!
>
> (5.1.261–262)

It is beyond dispute that an account or accounts of the first circumnavigation provided source material for *The Tempest* – it is only the extent of Shakespeare's debt that is open to question. Caliban is not a giant, and South America is not an island. We must still find Caliban, a deformed man living alone on a remote island, as Caliban was until the arrival of Prospero and Miranda on the island of the play. It is essential that the island is remote; there are no further visitors to Shakespeare's island for around twelve years after Prospero and Miranda are cast up there, an unlikely prospect for an island ostensibly set in the Mediterranean – but which we do not find in Patagonia either. We must look elsewhere.

IV

We Must Prepare to Meet with Caliban

Caliban has been described as the core of the play;[61] without him, we do not have the island of *The Tempest*. His most notable, but largely unspecified, physical characteristic is that he is deformed. This much we know from the 'Names of the Actors' in the First Folio, the earliest collected edition of Shakespeare's plays, published in 1623.[62] Although an actor must play Ariel's part, the character is not a person; he is 'an airy spirit'.[63] By contrast, Caliban is human, however low he might seem to be in the scheme of things. He has been portrayed on stage as an ape swinging in a tree, a monster with fins, and much worse, but he is a man: there is no doubt about this. Had Prospero not prevented his attempted violation of Miranda's 'honour' (1.2.348), Caliban claims that he would have 'peopled else/this isle with Calibans' (1.2.350–351). It was the *island* that was not honoured with a human shape – other than that of Caliban: Sycorax was dead and the arrival of Prospero and Miranda was still awaited. The punctuation in the Folio, if not in some later editions, is precise on this.[64]

Miranda provides further confirmation of Caliban's human status when she first sees Ferdinand:

> This is the third man that e'er I saw, the first
> That e'er I sighed for.
> (1.2.281–283)

Miranda has previously seen Prospero and Caliban. Now she sees Ferdinand. All are men.

But Caliban is a 'savage and deformed slave'[65] and should be played as such. The problem is that that we have almost no information about his deformities, hence the myriad representations of these on stage. The text of the play gives us few genuine clues, and, as Morton Luce, editor of the first Arden edition of *The Tempest*, put it in 1901:

> If all the suggestions as to Caliban's form and feature and endowments that are thrown out in the play are collected, it will be found that the one half renders the other half impossible.[66]

The only certainty to be derived from what Shakespeare wrote, as opposed to what others have imposed on the text, is that Caliban has long fingernails:

> And I with my long nails will dig thee pignuts,
> (2.2.168)

When Prospero calls Caliban a tortoise, it is because he is slow; when he is called a fish, it is because of his smell. Caliban should not be portrayed as a tortoise or a fish. To be true to what was written, we should forget about fins and focus on his fingernails. Humans have fingernails, but there has been little, if any, effort to link Shakespeare's inspiration for the creation of Caliban with a real person. As we will see, however, there was a man who may have been the prototype Caliban.

To be the island of *The Tempest* there must be a Caliban on it. Bermuda does not provide us with this essential. As Alden T. Vaughan and Virginia Mason Vaughan note in *Shakespeare's Caliban: A Cultural History*:

> There were no natives on Bermuda, so the shipwrecked party's experience and the several accounts of it cannot be direct sources.[67]

To find Caliban, we must return to the accounts of Magellan's voyage.

V

This Island's Mine

It is fairly certain that the first circumnavigators did not call at Saint Helena. Magellan's *Victoria*, by then under the command of Juan Sebastián de Elcano, rounded the Cape of Good Hope and next made land at Santiago, in the Cape Verde Islands, where a number of men were abandoned when an attack was feared. Only eighteen of the two hundred and sixty-eight men who had set out in Magellan's fleet were on board the *Victoria*, the only vessel of the fleet to return, when it reached Spain on 6 September 1522. But these were not the only survivors of the expedition: others got home in due course, including those left behind at Santiago. Pigafetta's is not the only account of the voyage; or, in the case of those who arrived back after him, what may better be described as the several voyages resulting in their eventual return. We also have the *Narrative of a Portuguese companion of Odoardo Barbosa, in the ship Victoria, in the year 1519*, which appears in Giovanni Battista Ramusio's *Delle navagationi e viaggi*. Ramusio was a Venetian diplomat whose duties gave him access to accounts of overseas exploration from a wide range of sources.

Odoardo Barbosa, who is referred to in the narrative's title, was Magellan's brother-in-law. Like Magellan, Barbosa did not survive the venture, but his unnamed companion evidently did; although, he was not on the *Victoria* when it returned to Spain, nor was he one of those left behind in Santiago – this is clear from his narrative. Probably, he was one of those who had stayed in the East Indies when the *Victoria* sailed for home. It follows from this that his voyage back was on a different ship, almost certainly a Portuguese one. This explains the following passage in his narrative:

> If from the islands of Banda you wish to round the Cape of Good Hope, you must sail between west and south-west until you find yourselves in thirty-four degrees and a half of south latitude, and from there you sail westward, always keeping a look-out at the prow not to run aground on the said Cape of Good Hope or its neighbourhood. From this Cape of Good Hope one sails north-west by west 2400 miles, and there finds the island of St Helena, where Portuguese ships go to take in water and wood, and other things. The island is in sixteen degrees south latitude, and there is no habitation except that of a Portuguese man, who has but one foot, no nose, and no ears, and is called Fornam-lopem.

To discover more about Fornam-lopem and how he came to be the island's sole resident at the time of this account, we must look to events in India – where Afonso de Albuquerque had been sent to take charge of Portuguese interests in 1510.

Albuquerque may have failed in some of his more madcap schemes (a plan to bring Egypt to its knees by diverting the course of the Nile being one of them), but his achievements were enormous and included the taking of Malacca in 1511, in which Magellan took part. This provided the Portuguese with the key to the Moluccas and a way through to its lucrative spice trade. Goa had been colonized for this purpose and a Portuguese population established there through a calculated policy of intermarriage. But Goa had come under threat while Albuquerque was away securing Malacca. He returned to relieve it in 1512 and captured the fortress at Benastarim. The terms of the surrender included the delivery to Albuquerque of a number of Portuguese who had gone further than his policy had envisaged in integrating with Indian society. They had 'turned Turk' and, in so doing, become guilty of the twin crimes of apostasy and treason: converting to the Muslim faith and taking up arms against their Christian ruler. Their leader was Fornam-lopem, although Ramusio's rendering of his name appears to be unique. In Portuguese, it would have been Fernão Lopes. Generations of schoolchildren in Saint Helena have known him as Dom Fernando.

A condition of the handing over of the traitors – and, whatever sympathy one may have for their fate, this is what they were – insisted upon by the defeated Indian commander and agreed to by Albuquerque, was that their lives would be spared. But Albuquerque was being economical with the truth; they would only live if they survived his terrible retribution. Most of them did not. On the first day, their hair, beards, and eyebrows were pulled out, and they were dragged through mud mixed with pig excrement. On the second, their ears and noses were cut off. Finally, on the third day, they lost their right hands and left thumbs. Only then were dressings applied to their wounds.

We should pause to consider how much of this might be reflected in *The Tempest*. The subject of apostasy fascinated audiences of Shakespeare's time, and they were offered plays on the subject: *A Christian Turned Turk*, by Robert Daborne, appeared in 1612. Against this background, we begin to understand the significance of Sycorax in *The Tempest*, although, other than by reference, she does not appear in the play. Dying on the island, she leaves Caliban with a South American god. As we learn from Prospero, she had been banished from Algiers 'for mischiefs manifold and sorceries terrible' (1.2.264). Oddly, Prospero describes her as a 'blue eyed hag' (1.2.269). If there were any Patagonians in Algiers in this period, we have no record of them, and, when portraying North Africans, blue eyes do not quickly come to mind. There seems no obvious reason for blue eyes – which are normally associated with Europeans – to feature in what we know about Sycorax. To understand this, we need to know that the Algiers of the time was a hotbed of apostasy: by 1581, Christian 'renegades' made up more than half of the population there.[68] Sycorax is given a heathen god: she is, I suggest, a European who had abandoned her Christian faith. Caliban is the son of an apostate, and, arguably, he is one in his own right. We must assume that Prospero and Miranda have taught him Christianity and that Prospero is his Christian ruler, but Caliban conspires with Stephano and Trinculo to murder Prospero and seize the island.

Caliban's fate is not as awful as Dom Fernando's: when brought by Ariel to face justice before Prospero, he is (along with Stephano and Trinculo) led through a 'filthymantled pool' (4.1.182) from which they emerge, as Trinculo puts it, smelling 'all horse piss' (4.1.199). It does not take too much creative thinking to move from pig excrement to this. For those who want Caliban to be portrayed as a fish, we may note that the practice of tearing hair out by the roots, as happened with Dom Fernando, was known as 'scaling the fish'.[69] If we want Caliban to be a tortoise, Dom Fernando's appearance, minus his ears and nose, is apt enough to provide us (and Shakespeare) with such an image.

Albuquerque died in 1515, and Dom Fernando then gained a place on a ship bound for Portugal. In accordance with established practice, this ship called at Saint Helena. It was there that Dom Fernando decided he would travel no further, and he could not be found when it was time for the ship to set sail for Lisbon. Being commendably more charitable toward him than Albuquerque had been, his shipmates left him some food, a fire, a letter, and some of their own clothes. The letter asked him to show himself if any ship (almost inevitably, it would be a Portuguese one) arrived at the island so that he could be supplied with whatever he needed in order to survive there.

We may speculate as to why Dom Fernando jumped ship in Saint Helena – it may be that he feared further punishment in Portugal. More likely, he could not face returning there in his appalling condition. He had been born, if not into the nobility, at least into the gentry, and his wife might still have been optimistically looking forward to his return. Would he have wished to be seen by her as he now was? Life alone on Saint Helena suddenly held more appeal, and he set about providing himself with shelter:

> First of all, with the four fingers that remained to him and with the stump of his right arm, he scooped out a

sort of cave in the side of a soft bank of earth, in which to make his home...the mouth of which he guarded with prickly bushes.[70]

It is difficult not to think of Caliban's long fingernails, useful when carrying out excavations. Ariel's description of the protection given by natural materials to Prospero's 'poor cell' also comes to mind – 'the line-grove which weather-fends your cell' (5.1.10).

In spite of what had been urged upon him in the letter, Dom Fernando kept clear of visitors to the island, but they left him cheeses and other treats when they called. On one occasion he retrieved a cockerel from the sea – it had made its own break for freedom from a ship in the bay. In view of Dom Fernando's disabilities, his recovery of the bird was a considerable achievement. He kept it as a pet, his sole companion on the island, and slept with it beside him. As Trinculo states in the play, when first meeting Caliban and seeking cover under Caliban's gaberdine, 'Misery acquaints a man with / Strange bedfellows' (2.2.38–39).

Dom Fernando achieved what we would now call celebrity status:

> ...his fame spread far and wide and came at last to the ears of King John III, who sent a letter to Fernando promising him safe conduct if he would return to Portugal.[71]

And this is what Dom Fernando did. He travelled to Portugal, where King John III and Queen Catherine received him in private audience. His rehabilitation in his own country had commenced, and he was given a home (probably bringing with it an income) – 'a hermitage and a house of friars wherein he might remain.'[72]

But Dom Fernando had a pressing spiritual need, not sufficiently met by living with the friars. He needed to be freed of his sins.

VI

As You from Crimes Will Pardoned Be

There had been plenty of time in Saint Helena for Dom Fernando to reflect on his fall from grace, a more spiritual concept in Shakespeare's time than generally applies today. Back in Portugal, he resolved to do something about it. His king (the son of King Manuel, against whose rule he had risen in India) could forgive him, even honour him, but he could do little about Dom Fernando's crime against God. This was of such enormity that only one person on earth could help:

> So to Rome Lopez went and there at the foot of the Vicar of Christ the mutilated exile sobbed out the story of his transgressions, the double crime of apostasy and the taking up arms against a Christian people and there he received absolution.[73]

Dom Fernando, concerned that King John might prevent this, then told the pope of his wish to return to Saint Helena. The pope directed it, the king complied, and Dom Fernando saw out his days in Saint Helena, dying there in 1545.

The parallels with Caliban are striking. Caliban plots against his Christian ruler and is defeated. Prospero offers him his personal forgiveness:

> Go, sirrah, to my cell;
> Take with you your companions: as you look
> To have my pardon, trim it handsomely.
> (5.1.291–293)

Caliban responds as follows:

> Ay, that I will: and I'll be wise hereafter,
> And seek for grace.
> (5.1.294–295)

True redemption, in Caliban's case, seems to be a future event; wisdom and grace are to be part of a longer journey. The other characters of the play will soon be gone from the island – they will leave the next day. Simply trimming Prospero's cell in the meantime hardly appears sufficient penance to secure a return to grace. Prospero's pardon is at best temporal: no priest is among the characters of *The Tempest*, there is nobody who can grant absolution. There are priests elsewhere in Shakespeare's plays, but none in *The Tempest*. The audience is not told whether Caliban is to leave the island with the other characters or will remain behind to resume life alone on the island. One reading, particularly if Shakespeare had Dom Fernando in mind, is that Caliban is included in the voyage back to Naples but will later return to the island, freed from his sins, to be once again his 'own king' (1.2.343). Certainly, the pursuit of grace is so obvious a similarity that it considerably strengthens the case for Dom Fernando being the prototype Caliban. But we need a further connection with Saint Helena if we are to show it to be the island of the play – the presence of a suitable Caliban figure is not quite enough by itself. We need what a lawyer would call corroboration, some further evidence, independent of this, that it is indeed Shakespeare's island. A Prospero would do well for this.

VII

Rapt in Secret Studies

It has been much speculated that Shakespeare based the character of Prospero on John Dee – sometimes referred to as Dr John Dee, although there is no record of when and where he may have gained his doctorate. His credentials are perfect for the role. Dee was a polymath: a person who has knowledge of just about everything. He was an astrologer, alchemist, cryptographer, magician, and much more. Dee immersed himself in study and established what was then the greatest private library in England, perhaps in the whole of Europe. In total, he amassed close to four thousand books. To put this in perspective, it rivalled in terms of size the combined collections of the universities of Oxford and Cambridge at the time.

As an astrologer, Dee was tasked by Robert Dudley, the future Earl of Leicester, with identifying the most auspicious date for the coronation of Elizabeth I: Dudley had been given responsibility for organizing the event. After much study of the stars and planets, Dee came up with 15 January 1559, and it would seem that he did well in his commission – Elizabeth was to reign for more than forty-four years.

Alchemy was a less successful area for Dee, although he devoted a great deal of time and effort to it. In so doing, he attracted the attention of Ben Jonson, who names him in *The Alchemist*, a play first performed in 1610, a year or so before Shakespeare produced *The Tempest*:

He shall have a bell, that's Abel;
And, by it, standing one whose name is Dee,
In a rug gown; there's D and Rug, that's Drug:
And, right anenst him, a Dog snarling Er;
There's Drugger, Abel Drugger. That's his sign.
And here's now mystery, and hieroglyphic![74]

This gives us cryptography as well as alchemy. Dee presented his *Monas Hieroglyphica* to Queen Elizabeth at Greenwich Palace on 14 June 1564. The book was an almost impenetrable work based on coded mathematics. The 'rug gown' referred to by Jonson was one of a rough woollen material worn by those such as Dee who studied astrology and mathematics, perhaps like the one he is wearing in the portrait of him that survives and is now in the Ashmolean Museum, Oxford.

We should remember that Shakespeare was an actor as well as a writer, and that he performed in Jonson's plays. We know that he was in the cast of an early production of *Everyman in His Humour*, which, unlike the version of the play we are more familiar with today, then had an Italianate setting. The play had a character called Prospero. Jonson's Prospero has the line: 'No harm done, brother, I warrant you.' (4.3.7).[75] In *The Tempest*, Prospero assures Miranda: 'There's no harm done' (1.2.16). This could be a coincidence, but it seems unlikely; the same words are used by a character with the same name in each play. Shakespeare certainly borrowed Prospero's name from Jonson: but this may also be an example of his ability to remember and recycle a good line, often many years after the event. In addition, there is a Stephano in both the original version of *Everyman in His Humour* and *The Tempest*.

Shakespeare is more subtle than Jonson when bringing Dee into *The Tempest* – he does nothing so direct as name him. Dee was famous for his library and books were important to him. They were the key to everything, and his obsession with his studies brought him close to financial ruin through his expenditure on them. Prospero lost his position as 'the right Duke of Milan' because of his obsession with books (thus neglecting his duties as a ruler). It was when Prospero was 'rapt in secret studies' that Antonio was able to displace him.

The play emphasizes the power of books. Set adrift with Miranda in 'a rotten carcass of a butt' (1.2.146), Prospero receives from Gonzalo the precious gift that will eventually enable him to regain his position in Milan:

> Knowing I loved my books, he furnished me
> From mine own library with volumes that
> I prize above my dukedom.
>
> (1.2.166–168)

By devoting even more time to these on the island, Prospero achieves the power through his Art (his magic) to conjure up a storm and bring his enemies under his control. Caliban clearly identifies the danger to himself and his fellow conspirators, Stephano and Trinculo, when they set off to murder

Prospero – the success of their plot relies on them having 'first seized' (3.2.89) Prospero's books:

> Without them
> He's but a sot, as I am, nor hath not
> One spirit to command. They all do hate him
> As rootedly as I. Burn but his books.
> (3.2.92–95)

But Prospero prevails, and, as the play reaches its conclusion, he makes plans to return to Milan. He knows that he must now devote himself to his duties as a ruler, that his dukedom must be prized above his studies: his Art, having served its purpose, must be abandoned:

> But this rough magic
> I here abjure; and when I have required
> Some heavenly music (which even now I do)
> To work mine end upon their senses that
> This airy charm is for, I'll break my staff,
> Bury it certain fathoms in the earth,
> And deeper than did ever plummet sound
> I'll drown my book.
> (5.1.50–57)

Presumably this is in the singular so that he can hold a book, together with the staff, as he delivers these lines.

We have no record of Dee having drowned any books in the Thames or of him burying a magic staff, if he had one, but we do know that he buried books near the river at Mortlake. These were connected with his considerable interest in the occult and were dug up in the early seventeenth century by the antiquarian and collector Sir Robert Cotton. Still legible, although badly damaged by dampness, they were transcribed and published in 1659 as *A True and Faithful Relation of What Passed for Many Years Between Dr John Dee and Some Spirits*.[76] It seems obvious that Sir Robert did not dig at Mortlake on a whim; but we do not know what information, other than local rumour, he was acting on when he made his discovery. What is clear is that Dee's burial of his books was well known, at least in Mortlake, as it must have been in Shakespeare's time if information about the whereabouts of the books was to survive to Cotton a few years later. Shakespeare was well placed to know about the buried books. Augustine Phillips, a fellow sharer in the company to which Shakespeare belonged, had a house in Mortlake. In 1603, the King's Men, as they had recently become, gathered there prior to meeting their new patron, James I. The king's arrival in London, following his journey down from Scotland to succeed Queen Elizabeth I on the throne of England (he was already King of Scotland), had been delayed by an outbreak of plague in the city, and he was staying at Wilton House, near Salisbury, where he had temporarily established his court. We do not know how many times Shakespeare visited Mortlake, but this provides an almost certain instance. Phillips, the company's host in Mortlake, had – like Shakespeare – aspired to the status of a gentleman (bringing with it the entitlement to be addressed as 'Mister'), and, like Shakespeare, he had acquired a coat of arms to mark this. The other essential requirement was a suitable property, which is how he became a neighbour of John Dee. Mortlake was a fairly comfortable walk from London, and Phillips clearly found it congenial.

When the time came to move on to Wilton House, Shakespeare and his fellows received thirty pounds between them:

> for the paynes and expenses…in coming from Mortelake in the countie of Surrie unto the court aforesaid and there presenting before his majestie one playe.[77]

The company had become the King's Men on 19 May, when letters patent were issued licensing them to perform 'well for the recreation of our loving subjects, as for our solace and pleasure when we shall think good to see them'. They were now servants of the king and were appointed 'grooms of the chamber'. Along with this came a livery of doublet, hose, and cloak and participation in James's coronation procession. Shakespeare received four and a half yards of scarlet cloth for the occasion.

The period of enforced idleness at Mortlake provides an interesting possibility that Shakespeare had his portrait painted there. For those who believe the Sanders Portrait, now in Canada, to be of Shakespeare, we may at least reflect that it is dated 1603 and that it is in 1603 that Shakespeare had time to sit for it.

Because of Dee's diary, we have an extensive list of those who visited him at his home in Mortlake. Unfortunately, there is no mention among them of Shakespeare; nor is there any mention of any plays, by Shakespeare or anybody else, among the texts held in Dee's library, although we have an extensive inventory of the works that Dee owned. Visitors mentioned by Dee, however, include Thomas Cavendish, in 1590, who, as we have seen, had called at Saint Helena two years before – during his famous circumnavigation. Dee leaves us no detail of any conversation between them about the voyage, but common sense dictates that there must have been some talk of it. Dee simply notes the following in his diary (original spelling retained):

> May 18th, the two gentlemen, the unckle Mr. Richard Candish, and his nephew the most famous Mr. Thomas Candish, who had sayled rownd abowt the world, did viset me at Mortlake.[78]

Dee knew Richard Cavendish well, and he is mentioned several times in Dee's diary. They had a shared acquaintance in George Carey, the patron of both Thomas Cavendish and Shakespeare. Carey was godfather to Dee's daughter Madimi – and, when Dee sought the provostship of Eton College, Richard Cavendish and George Carey were the joint petitioners on his behalf.

We do not know what other contact Dee may have had with Thomas Cavendish, but voyagers were frequent visitors to Mortlake, as again evidenced by Dee's diary:

> Aug. 28th [1580], my dealing with Sir Humfrey Gilbert for his graunt of discovery.
>
> March 23rd [1581], at Mortlak cam to me Hugh Smyth, who had returned from Magellan straights and Vaygatz.
>
> June 17th [1581], yong Mr. Hawkins, who had byn with Sir Francis Drake, cam to me at Mortlake.

October 21st [1582], cam Mr. Clement the seamaster...

November 9th [1582], Mr Newbury, who had been at Cambaya in Inde, cam to me.[79]

Dee's library was an important resource centre, and its owner was a man to be consulted by those contemplating a voyage to distant lands. As important as the original instruction given to them by Dee was the feedback to him from returning voyagers, bringing new intelligence of the outside world. The accumulation of knowledge was incremental; Dee's was the best briefing to be had and, with each succeeding report back to him, it got better. When Martin Frobisher set off to search for a navigable northwest passage into the Pacific in 1576, he wrote to Dee from the Shetland Islands thanking him for his 'friendly Instructions: which when we use we do remember you'. Dee's knowledge, demonstrated if required from the contents of his library, astonished those who met him. William Bourne, author of *A Regiment for the Sea*, recalled such an occasion:

> As upon a time being with Master *Dee* at his house at *Murclacke*, we falling in talke about the discouerie to *Cattay* & so talked as touching the shipping.[80]

Dee then reached for a 'Booke' showing that 'the great *Cane*' (the ruler of China) had fifteen thousand ships. Bourne protested that surely these were 'small things'. Dee then 'turned unto another place' and showed that they were not. Bourne was clearly impressed – and his own book closes with this account.

Not all of the mariners calling at Mortlake, however, made a positive contribution. John Davis, the explorer credited with showing that Greenland is an island, actually set about stealing works from Dee's library!

In 1676, John Aubrey produced his *Brief Lives*.[81] There was, as he discovered on visiting Mortlake, one living link with Dee still remaining – 'old goodwife Faldo'. Aubrey interviewed her in 1672. She was 'eighty or more' but could remember Dee from when she was a child, although her recollections may well have been supplemented by rumour and gossip that lived on locally after Dee's death. Aubrey gives us the following from goodwife Faldo:

> She said he kept a great many stills going; that he laid the storm by magic; that the children dreaded him because he was accounted a conjuror.[82]

The reference to a storm almost jumps off the page at anybody looking for a Prospero. 'Laid' meant contrived – as we use it today in the expression 'the best laid plans'. Dee could, it seems, conjure up a storm, which must be a major requirement for a prospective Prospero.

Goodwife Faldo tells us that Dee was a conjuror, but his reputation on this score was considerable even without her account. It started with a theatrical performance early in his life. Dee went to Cambridge in 1542, to Saint John's College. He subsequently became a founding fellow of Trinity College, where he was a reader in Greek and put on a performance of Aristophanes's *Peace*. This requires Trygaeus, a 'vine dresser', to ascend to Zeus's heavenly palace. A ladder being insufficient for the purpose, the good offices of a dung beetle are required. As Dee achieved it, the creature rose with Trygaeus on its back and a 'great wondering' spread through the audience. This was of course nothing more than an illusion – magic of the sort that we regard as entertainment today. But the effect on the audience, produced by little more than pulleys, mirrors, and a significant element of surprise, was remarkable: some are said to have fled the hall. The rising of the dung beetle brings to mind similar effects in *The Tempest*. Among these are when Ariel:

> ...claps his wings upon the table, and with a quaint device the banquet vanishes.
> (Stage direction following 3.3.52)

Shakespeare's plays were mostly performed in daylight, and illusions, such as that of the disappearing banquet, would have been difficult, but not impossible, to achieve during the afternoon performances at *The Globe*. By 1611, however, there was an alternative: performances indoors, lit by candles. The theatre at the Blackfriars was very different to those south of the Thames, and it catered to a more sophisticated and better off clientele. Seats here cost serious money, and those who were prepared to pay sixpence for one expected the sort of spectacle that would justify such a price. Productions at *The Globe* had always been, and continued to be, continuous, with beer, nuts, and other commodities sold to the audience as plays progressed; but there were breaks at the Blackfriars, as we now expect when we go to the theatre. We owe the existence of the intervals that we now enjoy to the intermittent need to trim the candles at the Blackfriars.

The case for Dee being the inspiration for Prospero is obvious, and there must have been those in the audience who thought of him when they saw a performance of *The Tempest* at the Blackfriars. The play has plenty of what we would now call special effects; even the storm is an illusion. Prospero is a conjuror, and he lays the storm. But beyond being a man who had met Cavendish, did Dee have any real connection with Saint Helena?

The Environs of London: Volume 1: County of Surrey, by Daniel Lysons, was published in 1792. Lysons dealt in some detail with Mortlake and its most famous resident, emphasizing the wide range of Dee's interests and achievements:

> He wrote upon the reformation of the Gregorian calendar, on the mode of propagating the Gospel on the other side of the Atlantic; on geography; astrology; and the occult sciences. He wrote also of his voyage to St. Helena.[83]

So here we have it, the earliest suggestion, I believe, that Dee travelled to Saint Helena. It was carried over into just about every account of Dee's life written over the next two hundred years. The sources cited by Lysons in his book do not show where he got this from, but the 1888 entry in the *Dictionary of National Biography* is more helpful. It states that:

> At some period of his life Dee visited St. Helena, and wrote an account of his voyage (AYSCOUGH, Cat. OF MSS p.873; Cotton MS, Appendix xlvi, 2 parts).

The *Ayscough Catalogue*, compiled in 1782 and thus available to Lysons when he wrote *The Environs of London*, may be seen at the British Library. The *Catalogue* refers to the journal twice. At page 687, we have:

> Journal of a voyage to St Helen's in 1582, containing some draughts and curious observations. Qe. By John Dee, author of conference with angels.

Later, at page 873, under 'Magic and Witchcraft', appears the following:

> A quantity of folio paper-books of his own hand-writing, consisting of many parts of his Liber Mysterium, and conferences with angels.
> Diarium Oxon. 1582. In this is the journal of a voyage to St. Helena, with some curious observations.

The 'journal of a voyage to St. Helena', like the *Ayscough Catalogue*, is now kept at the British Library. There can be no doubt that this is what we are looking for. It describes itself on its first page as 'Diarium Oxon. 1582.' There is also a note, dating from 1854, stating that 'the contents of this volume were formerly kept with the unbound papers of Dr John Dee.'[84] Dee had possession of the journal and would have been better able than most to read and understand its contents – it contains passages in Greek, Latin, and cipher. Dee was fluent in both languages and, as we have seen, was a noted cryptographer. It was kept in his library at Mortlake, but he did not write it; it was written by Richard Madox, a minister of religion. The diary contains an account of a voyage into the Atlantic under the command of Edward Fenton. Madox was one of the two chaplains who participated in the venture. It is Edward Fenton who provides us with our second link between Saint Helena and *The Tempest*.

VIII

When It Is Bak'd with Frost

Edward Fenton was a resident of Deptford, now a part of south-east London. It is difficult to picture Deptford as a town in its own right, as it once was, separated from the capital by several miles of countryside. But the broad, muddy sweep of the Thames, with Deptford Creek joining it from the south, provides some continuity. Henry VIII established a dockyard here in 1513, close to his favourite palace, Greenwich, from which he could keep watch on the building and equipping of his fleet. He could also banquet on the vessels as they prepared to sail.

Saint Nicholas's Church – which houses a memorial to Fenton – is at the junction of Deptford Green and the quaintly named Stowage. The memorial is unusual in that Fenton's epitaph was added to it many years after his death. Originally, it seems, the monument of which it is now a part was simply to Roger Boyle, a young boy who died in 1615. Roger, a bookish lad, is said, in the inscription relating to him, to have died of a surfeit of study, a warning much heeded by many subsequent generations of schoolchildren. Fenton, perhaps less burdened by the pursuit of academic excellence (although in 1569 he did contribute a translation of Pierre *Boaistau's Certaine Secrete wonders of Nature* to the canon of English literature), had lived to a reasonable age and is presented on the memorial as something of a national hero:

> Richard Earl of Cork erected this well-deserved monument to his wife's paternal uncle. To the perpetual memory of Edward Fenton, formerly Esquire of the body to Queen Elizabeth, and who afterwards served with great distinction as Brigadier in the civil commotions occasioned by Shane O'Neil, and afterwards by the Earl of Desmond, in Ireland. He subsequently undertook many bold and adventurous voyages in the unknown seas of the Far North exploring previously uninhabited regions. Finally he commanded the Admiral's flagship in the famous naval engagement against the Spanish Armada. He died in 1603.[85]

This, a translation from the original Latin, contains a remarkable amount of information. We know from it that Fenton was a gentleman of the guard to Queen Elizabeth I and that he captained the *Mary Rose* ('the Admiral's flagship') at the time of the Armada. These are impressive credentials. He also saw military service in Ireland and 'undertook many bold and adventurous voyages in the unknown seas of the Far North'. These voyages were with Martin Frobisher; we will return to them later.

Apart from the epitaph and the six lines of rhyme that follow it (which include a reference to Fenton's 'high renown'), there is little else about the monument that seems, at first sight, to have much to do with Fenton. Young Roger is shown in sculpted alabaster, with figures representing youth and death skulking under a canopy behind him. He is kneeling, in prayer or contemplation, a book open before him. It is what can best be described as a carving within a carving, framed like a picture or a view through a window, that relates to Fenton. It shows three ships, on what could be a river, an estuary, or a strait. The land seen on either side is like a map in relief, too distinct in its features to have been left entirely to the imagination of the sculptor. There are several buildings on one side, a single one on the other. These are of a style similar to those then flanking the tidal Thames, but could equally represent English buildings erected elsewhere, perhaps in a settlement in 'the Far North'. This will make more sense when we learn more about Fenton.

Fenton moved in high circles. His younger brother, Sir Geoffrey Fenton, was secretary of state for Ireland. Sir Geoffrey's daughter Katherine married Richard Boyle, a union that produced Roger, their eldest son, the lad who died in 1615. Richard Boyle became the Earl of Cork, as he is styled in the introductory words about Fenton on the memorial, on 26 October 1620. It follows that the memorial, or at least the part of it that relates to Fenton, cannot have been installed before then. Why this belated recognition of Fenton's achievements? Perhaps it was a desire by Boyle to plump up his family history a bit, to elevate it to one befitting his new status as an earl. On the evidence of his epitaph, Fenton was perfect for this purpose.

In fact, the real Fenton was not one of the sixteenth century's great success stories. But we need to look at the voyages he undertook with Frobisher in order to see how close he came to an achievement which, had it been fulfilled, would have left him famous to this day.

Frobisher made three voyages to what is now Canada: in 1576, 1577, and 1578. The first voyage, in which Fenton did not participate, had only one purpose: to find a northwest passage to the Pacific – 'the onely thing of the Worlde that was left yet undone, whereby a notable mind mighte be made famous and fortunate.'[86]

The voyagers did not find a way through to the Pacific, but they did return home with a piece of rock that they believed (wrongly) to contain gold. A further voyage, largely financed in reliance upon this, was planned for the following year. The fleet was to be a larger one, with the Queen's ship the *Ayde* added to the *Gabriel* and the *Michael*. This is where Edward Fenton enters – he was appointed captain of the *Gabriel*. No longer was the mission to search for a new route to China; the fleet's task was to return with more of the seemingly gold-bearing ore. With this in mind, eight miners from the Forest of Dean were recruited, an exercise largely carried out by Fenton. A great deal of ore was brought back, but, when no gold was found in it, the existing facilities for its extraction in England were deemed to be at fault: it was unthinkable that there *was* no gold. A proper processing plant, to be established at Dartford, on the south bank of the tidal Thames, was considered to be the answer. To provide still more raw material for this facility, an even larger fleet was assembled for the 1578 voyage, consisting of the *Ayde, Gabriel, Michael, Judith, Thomas Allen, Hopewell, Anne Frances, Thomas of Ipswich, Frances of Foye, Moon of Foye*, and, a late addition, the *Beare Leicester*.

Edward Fenton was appointed captain of the *Judith*, and to be Frobisher's lieutenant general; but he had also been selected for a further role, the one that would have secured him a lasting place in history had it come to anything. A colony was to be established on Countess of Warwick Island,[87] and Fenton was to have charge of it. Had he succeeded, the colony would have preceded Raleigh's in Roanoke, North Carolina, by ten years.

Most of what was required for the colony on Countess of Warwick Island would have to be taken there in the ships, including what has been described as a 'prefabricated blockhouse'.[88] This would provide both shelter and security. Frobisher had claimed that there was a need to both occupy and fortify what was now, in English eyes at least, a possession of Queen Elizabeth I. The provisioning for the one hundred prospective colonists, all of them men, was impressive, if by modern standards unbalanced, including 133 tons of beer (four pints per man per day), one pound of cheese per man per day, and four hundred bushels of peas – the only vegetable. Most of the peas were destined to go into permanent cold storage on the island.

The fleet encountered appalling weather conditions, the worst by far of any of the three voyages. The ships were dispersed and what remained of them (the *Denys*, holed by an iceberg, was lost, and the *Thomas of Ipswich* ran for home) did not reassemble for seven weeks. In an effort to avoid the fate of the *Denys*, the crews of the other vessels protected themselves from the ice with whatever best served the purpose, including component parts of the blockhouse. This was to prove fatal to the establishment of a colony.

The *Ayde* anchored off Countess of Warwick Island on July 30, but Fenton had arrived there first and set up camp – Frobisher dined with him on the *Judith* that evening. Pending more permanent repair, a hole in the *Ayde* was plugged with a side of beef. There is no record of any discussion about the proposed colony until 9 August, when it transpired that the materials for its main building had been separately stowed on several of the ships – the lost *Denys* being one of them. With the splintered spars (used to fend off the ice) taken into account, this seemed to rule out staying on the island for an Arctic winter. Undaunted, Fenton suggested a scaled down settlement, with only sixty men, with whom he was prepared to spend the next few months. Realistically, nobody who chose to remain was likely to survive the experience. Sensibly, Frobisher overruled Fenton. Little time was left before winter would set in, and food stocks were now running alarmingly low. Fenton noted on 22 August that among the limited supplies left there were only two hundred and fifty 'poor John' (dried fish) on the *Ayde*. We may speculate that by now they had 'a very ancient and fish-like smell, a kind of – not of the newest – poor-John' (2.2.25–26), the very thought of which Shakespeare was to appall his audience with in *The Tempest*. Only a gesture to represent the proposed colony was now possible, and Fenton supervised the construction of a small building, traces of which may still be seen today. As described by Thomas Ellis, of the *Ayde*:

> Before we took shipping, we built a little house in the Countess of Warwick's Island, and garnished it with many kinds of trifles, as pins, points, laces, glasses, combs, babes on horseback and on foot, with

innumerable other such fancies and toys, thereby to allure and entice the people to some familiarity against other years.[89]

But there were to be no other years on the island for the builders of the little house, nor was any other European to visit the island during the next three hundred years.[90]

Things had not gone to plan as far as establishing a colony was concerned, but Ellis was in no doubt as to Fenton's heroic intent:

> I will turn my pen a little to Master Captain Fenton, and those Gentlemen which should have inhabited all the year in those countries, whose valiant minds were much to be commended, that neither fear of force, nor the ripping storms of the raging winter, neither the temperature of so unhealthful a country, neither the savageness of the people, neither the sight and show of such and so many strange meteors, neither the desire to return to their native soil, neither regard of friends, neither care of possessions and inheritances, finally, not the love of life (a thing of all other most sweet), neither the terror of dreadful death itself, might seem to be of sufficient force to withdraw their prowess, or to refrain from that purpose, thereby to have profited their country, but that with most willing hearts, venturous minds, stout stomachs, and singular manhood, they were content there to have tarried for the time, among a barbarous and uncivilised people, infidels and miscreants, to have made their dwelling, not terrified with the manifold and imminent dangers which

they were like to run into; and seeing before their eyes so many casualties, whereto their life was subject, the least whereof would have made a milksop Thersites astonished and utterly discomfited, being, I say, thus minded and purposed, they deserved special commendation, for, doubtless, they had done as they intended, if luck had not withstood their willingness, and if that fortune had not so frowned upon their intents.[91]

This is not just a narrative; it is powerful poetry: 'neither fear of force, nor the ripping storms of the raging winter'. The alliteration hammers out images of epic courage.

But fortune frowned and Fenton was denied his colony. All that was left of the enterprise was a token of possession – the building, along with its contents, apparently intended to impress the local people. Fenton's ambition to establish a colony was, however, to surface again in a later enterprise, and in different waters.

IX

Had I Plantation of This Isle

We must now return to the diary written by Richard Madox, kept among Dee's papers at Mortlake. It is this diary that we largely rely upon for what is known about a later voyage by Edward Fenton. Madox was born on 11 November 1546, probably at Uffington in Shropshire, a place he later 'drempte muche of'. He attended Shrewsbury School, where the curriculum required that 'the top form had not only to read but to play an act of comedy once a week.'[92] There was nothing unusual about this; the success of the boy actor companies in London during Shakespeare's time reflected this tradition. Shakespeare even referred to them in his plays, perhaps with a tinge of commercial jealousy, as in *Hamlet*:

> There is, sir, an eyrie of children, little eyases, that cry out on top of question, and are most tyrannically clapped for't. They are now the fashion, and so berattle the common stages – so they call them – that many wearing rapiers are afraid of goose-quills and dare scarce come thither.[93]

Richmond Barbour, in his *The Third Voyage Journals*, an account of the third voyage of ships of the English East India Company, suggests that the practice of playing dramas in the schools assisted in putting on plays at sea, or, at least, in rest periods while at anchor during voyages, there being men on board who had received this sort of education. We have looked, in this book, at an account of a performance of *Hamlet* on board a ship of the East India Company; a ship that had, on an earlier voyage, called at Saint Helena.

After Shrewsbury, Madox attended All Souls College, Oxford, and became a priest. A brief summary of the main events in his life is annexed to his diary. Written in Latin, it shows that he lived at Dorchester, in Dorset, for a little less than three years, commencing on 15 July 1576, and that he made a trip to Paris in 1579, returning to Dorchester later that year. Had it not been for his diary, his literary fame would have rested entirely on a 'short, sweet and comfortable sermon' that he preached at Melcombe Regis, Dorset, in October 1581. This was published after his death by Thomas Martin, later recorded as the Town Clerk of Weymouth and Melcombe Regis, but it also seems to have appeared in print soon after its original delivery[94] – which was at a civic event of some importance, with the mayor, bailiffs, and aldermen of the joint borough in attendance. The sermon's subject was the sea. In only five lines, Madox managed to refer to 'sails of heavenly hope', the 'wind of God's spirit', 'the rudder of wisdom', the 'anchor of faith, and the 'mainmast of an upright conscience'.[95] However uplifting all of this might have been, he did not omit reference also to the dangers posed by the sea, including the risk of being 'eaten up' by it and suffering a 'miserable shipwreck'.[96] Madox may well have chosen his theme in an effort to establish his credentials for what lay ahead of him: he probably already knew that he had been selected as a chaplain to take part in the first English trading voyage to the Moluccas, the Spice Islands. This enterprise was intended to build on the contacts and goodwill established by Drake in the East Indies during his epic circumnavigation, completed the previous year. Drake was considered for the leadership of the fresh expedition, but tensions with Spain were rising fast and he was too valuable a commodity as a national hero to be placed at risk. Frobisher was chosen in his place.

Madox started his diary on New Year's Day, 1582, commencing with a quotation from the book of Jeremiah. This describes the revelation to the imprisoned prophet of how shepherds and their flocks would come into possession of a desolate land, a land without man or beast, a land cleared by the Almighty for occupation by the Godly. It would be easy to read too much into this choice of a prefatory text, but difficult not to note in it a perceived justification for colonialism. Madox was to set off on his adventure with 'a licence to preach in all the world'.[97] It was a world in which a heathen ruler had no proper place, one in which it was the duty of a Christian to convert or dispossess him. As Sir Humphrey Gilbert's commission for the voyage to Newfoundland put it in 1583, he was 'to inhabit and possess at his choice all remote and heathen lands not in the actual possession of any Christian prince.'[98]

This tells us a lot about the religion and politics of the time – two concepts then largely inseparable. A Catholic ruler (otherwise entitled to a land under the Treaty of Tordesillas) might not be regarded as a Christian by Protestants from England; but, if this argument failed, a Christian ruler might have his title defeated by reason of not being in 'actual' possession. English expansionism was on its way.

On 8 January 1582, as we learn from his diary, Madox attended a performance of George Gascoigne's translation of Ariosto's *I Suppositi*, which left him unmoved. He describes with far greater enthusiasm a 'clubbing' earlier in the day, an event involving a drum, bagpipes, garlands, orations, and the capture of a 'savage' who duly 'yelded his hollyn club'.[99] This was more to Madox's taste, and he reports it (including his own role in the event) with considerable enthusiasm. This excitement over, on 11 January Madox set off for London for a meeting with the Earl of Leicester. It was the earl who had secured Madox's release from his academic duties so that he could participate in the voyage:

> To my loving friends the Warden and Officers of All Souls in Oxford, after my hearty commendations, whereas Mr Madox, Fellow of your college, is presently to be employed in public affairs into far parts without this realm, from whence he is likely to return in two or three years or more, therefore do heartily pray and also require you that he may have a cause of three years absence from the college allowed him, and that his absence for the said time be no hindrance to his commodity in the college, but that he may enjoy all benefits thereof as if he were present, and so I bid you heartily farewell.
>
> Your very loving friend Rob Leicester[100]

This gives us a moment to reflect on the pecking order of Elizabethan society. Leicester was Chancellor of Oxford

University, and his request could hardly be refused. But he both *prays* and requires that Madox be released for the duration of the enterprise. This was the protocol of the time.

Madox was in London again by 19 February, when he visited the eminent compass maker Robert Norman. He also found time to go to the theatre, perhaps *the* Theatre (simply named that) in Shoreditch, built by James Burbage in 1576, where, on 22 February, he saw 'a scurvie play set owt al by one virgin which ther proved a fyemartin with *out* voice so that we stayd not the matter.'[101] The original spelling is so charming that I have retained it. How can one render 'fyemartin' in modern English? It seems that Madox, and whoever accompanied him to the play, left before the end of the performance. The full flowering of Elizabethan drama was still awaited.

Burbage's company of actors, like Madox, enjoyed the patronage of Leicester, and Burbage's players were called Leicester's Men. This demonstrates the immense power and extent of patronage in Elizabethan England. Leicester could protect a group of actors, nominate a chaplain for a voyage to the Spice Islands and, as the queen's favourite, be a pivotal figure in much else besides.

On 27 February, Madox noted in his diary: 'M. Furbusher was discharged of the viage and M. Fenton put in his place.' He writes nothing more of this. The reason for Frobisher's removal (or resignation) is not known.

Fenton's fleet set sail in May. It comprised only four ships: the *Galleon Leicester*, the *Edward Bonaventure*, the tiny *Bark Francis*, and another slightly larger bark, the *Elizabeth*. The fleet's complement totalled 235 men, a dozen or so of whom had circumnavigated the globe with Drake. These included the pilots of the *Galleon Leicester* and *Edward Bonaventure*.

John Drake captained his famous cousin's vessel, the *Bark Francis*. Fenton would have been less than human if he had been possessed of any ambition other than to emulate the great Sir Francis Drake, knighted by Elizabeth on board the *Golden Hind* at Deptford the year before.

Madox was the registrar for the voyage. As such, he kept an official account of it. But it is his unofficial account, his personal diary, with which we are concerned here. He was well aware that it would be confiscated on his return if found – everything concerning the voyage belonged to its backers – and he went to considerable lengths to maintain its confidentiality: he wrote parts in Latin and Greek, which probably protected its contents from examination by most of his shipmates. The most sensitive entries he wrote in cipher, which in all likelihood explains how it ended up in Dee's library at Mortlake – to be decoded. By way of additional security, when the ships reached Sierra Leone, he commenced writing some passages as if he was setting out the details of a play. As with the 'scurvie' play in London, he gives no title for it, but he does provide us with an author and a *dramatis personae*:

> Similarly in Aulus Gellius there is evidence of an elegant and witty comedy in which the leading role is played by Clodius, the second by Titus Annius Milo, the third by Glaucus who was acting in place of Clodius...There were also two servants, Verres, a notable and open thief, and Galba, a boasting buffoon.[102]

Several of these characters represent members of the expedition. Clodius, for example, is a pseudonym for Fenton, but Verres and Galba are not linked with any of those in the fleet. In *The Tempest*, the comic characters are Stephano and Trinculo: a 'drunken butler' and a 'jester' – the descriptions given to them in the First Folio.[103] Stephano is a thief, easily diverted from the plot to kill Prospero when Ariel enters, 'loaden with glistering apparel.' Stephano orders Trinculo to remove a gown so that he may have it. Trinculo is a jester, another name for a buffoon – which is Madox's description of Galba. Madox's Verres and Galba are servants, as are Stephano and Trinculo.

A True Declaration of the Estate of the Colonie in Virginia, a pamphlet dating from 1610, has been taken seriously by some as a hint to Shakespeare to pen *The Tempest*; it contains a reference to 'this tragicall Comaedie'.[104] Madox's 'elegant and witty comedy' seems worthy of similar consideration. The names Verres and Galba are both found in Thomas Wilson's *The Arte of Rhetorique*, first published in 1553 and reprinted in 1580. That Madox was familiar with the book is evident from his diary, in which he twice refers to it. He writes:

> I told them the land was nothing so unholsom as yt was heald but no persuasion in any thing can prevayle til need come to play the orator which rather useth Carters lodgique than Wilsons rhetorique.[105]

Later, there is an allusion to a story told by Wilson concerning a 'Book of Fools'. In *The Arte of Rhetorique*, such a book is kept by a jester. Madox does not name the jester, but he does name the king: 'Alphonsus king of Naples had a Jester in his Court.'

'Alphonsus' is a variant of 'Alonso', just as 'Furbisher' is of 'Frobisher', 'Candish' is of 'Cavendish', and 'Shakspere' is of

77

'Shakespeare'. In *The Tempest*, Alonso is King of Naples, and the storm deposits both him and his jester on the island, but coincidence must be linked with something more concrete. It may simply be that Madox and Shakespeare read the same books; there were less to read then than there are now. It is what happened in Sierra Leone, as Fenton frittered away the chance of seeing the enterprise through to its directed purpose, that is of such importance.

On 11 September, Madox made the following entry in his diary – in cipher:

> The general told me about the island of St Helena, lying between the equator and the tropic. He said it was a very fertile country and almost completely uninhabited, a place moreover easy and convenient to fortify, and having constructed defences, to plant a colony...and there we could await the return of the Portuguese fleet, which, laden with spices, touches there to water in the month of May.[106]

Considering that Cavendish had yet to visit and report on the attributes of the island, Fenton was remarkably well informed about it. Saint Helena, with its towering cliffs and few landing spots, was awaiting its moment to be transformed into a fortress. It was uninhabited, and it was fertile. It was suitable for settlement, and the Portuguese fleet did gather there in May, taking water from the Run before setting off on the last leg of the journey back from the Indies. Fenton would have had eight months in which to establish his colony – more than adequate for the purpose denied him on Countess of

Warwick Island in 1578. According to William Hawkins, Fenton's lieutenant, Fenton's plan was clear:

> The xxvith of Septembre 1582 Master Walker tolde me that he had a matter to let me know if I wolde not make it knowen: saying that the voyage we were come in was broken cleane, and that from oure first departure from England they weare determined not to proceede in that voyage of their device which never weare out of sight of their owne chimneys, or from their mothers pappes in respect of voyaging. In replie wheareof he said that the general was determined to enter in St Helena, and to possesse the same, and there to be proclaimed King, promising great rewards to all the well-willers who would consent to the same: as first to Captaine Warde £10,000, to Captaine Parker £5000, to Mr Walker £2,000 and to Mr Maddocks £2000. And for payment of this money he was determined to have taken the Portuguese Armathos if he coulde.[107]

We have, unequivocally, a man who wished to seize an island, establish a colony there, and become its king. If we need corroboration of this, it is borne out by other accounts from those who were there. Thomas Percy, shipmaster of the *Edward Bonaventure*, gave evidence at an enquiry back in England that Fenton had proposed to go to Saint Helena and 'inhabit' it,[108] and Peter Jeffery, a young merchant on board the same ship, confirmed this in his narrative of the voyage.[109] Luke Ward, the vice-admiral, left a record of the key events of the voyage, including Fenton's intentions concerning Saint Helena.[110]

What do we find of this in *The Tempest*? Shakespeare gives us the following in the play:

> GONZALO   Had I plantation of this isle, my lord –
>
> ANTONIO   He'd sow't with nettle-seed.
>
> SEBASTIAN Or dock's or mallows.
>
> GONZALO   And were the king on't, what would I do?
>
> SEBASTIAN 'Scape being drunk, for want of wine.
> (2.1.143–147)

To rule out mere coincidence, we may note that there was want of wine confronting Fenton's fleet, as explained by Elizabeth Story Donno, in *An Elizabethan in 1582*:

> At this point Fenton seems to have been vacillating between returning to the Cape Verde Islands or heading for St Helena. The following day he talked privately to Walker [the chaplain on the *Edward Bonaventure*] about returning to the Islands, arguing that unless they obtained a store of wine, the voyage would be utterly overthrown.[111]

Saint Helena had water in abundance, but no wine was awaiting any ship that might arrive there.[112]

We tend to forget that *The Tempest* is a comedy – chiefly because there is little in it that an audience today finds side-splittingly funny, although it has its moments if well performed, including when Trinculo creeps under Caliban's gaberdine in order to shelter from a storm.[113] Comedy is largely based on a shared cultural understanding, including a knowledge of current or at least still remembered recent events. We need to know *why* something is funny in order to be able to join in the laughter. Shakespeare's audience would have seen immediately what we can now only reconstruct. But humour explained is humour lost, although it remains interesting to see what was considered to be funny in Shakespeare's time. The balance of Gonzalo's speech, one of the most famous in the play, is drawn from Michel Montaigne's *Of the Canibales*. Montaigne wrote on a wide variety of subjects. His essays (he is widely credited with having introduced the essay form) were translated into English by John Florio in 1603.

Shakespeare did not, however, simply make great verse out of Montaigne's essay – there is humour here if we can but see it. It is noteworthy that Montaigne makes no mention in *Of the Canibales* of planting a colony and that he describes the people of whom he writes as having *no* rulers: 'no name of magistrate, nor of politike superiorite'. Shakespeare's adaptation of Montaigne is dependent for its effect on his audience knowing what he did *not* draw from *Of the Canibales* – this is where the amusement lies. In the play, the humour is turned against Gonzalo, but, for those familiar with Fenton's story, it is also aimed at Fenton. How many men were there in Shakespeare's time that planned to plant a colony and become its king? How many (if there were any others) ran out of wine during their endeavours? Against this background, the suggested perfection of Gonzalo's proposed government, which he claimed would 'excel the Golden Age'[114] (again not drawn from Montaigne) falls into place. The purpose of Fenton's first attempted colony was to mine what was believed to be gold-bearing ore: a belief based on nothing at all – and that became the subject of public ridicule. The purpose of his South Atlantic voyage was to emulate Drake, the Golden Knight, and again he failed. But the essential element for present purposes remains the singularity of his plan to plant a colony and become its king.

We have not a jot of evidence that Shakespeare ever saw Madox's diary. He may have, but we cannot show that he did. There may have been an opportunity at Mortlake in 1603, but there is nothing to show that this came to anything. As we have seen, however, there were other accounts of Fenton's voyage, including those of Hawkins, Thomas Percy, Peter Jeffery, and Luke Ward, cited above. We also have oral tradition, perhaps more important in Shakespeare's time than in our own. This was a story that almost certainly 'did the rounds' in London.

There is more, however, and we need to look again at the text of the play. Shakespeare had surgery on his mind when contriving the buildup to Gonzalo's speech:

GONZALO   You rub the sore
When you should bring the plaster.

SEBASTIAN   Very well.

ANTONIO   And most chirurgeonly!
(2.1.139–142)

A 'chirurgeon', in Shakespeare's time, was a surgeon – it was still evolving into the word we know today. Two surgeons were engaged on Fenton's voyage. The more eminent of these was John Banister. He was on the *Galleon Leicester*. The surgeon on the *Edward Bonaventure* was Lewis Otmore. We are able to trace both of these. Banister was, and remains, relatively famous: he warrants a place in the *Oxford Dictionary of National Biography*, which tells us that he lived in Silver Street, London, where Shakespeare lodged with the Mountjoy family between 1603 and 1607. Although Banister wrote several learned works, including *Antidoterie Chirurgical* (in which he refers to his residence in Silver Street), he is best remembered today for the 'anatomies'. These fascinated Shakespeare, as in King Lear: 'Let them anatomize Regan, see what breeds about her heart.'[115] In a portrait dating from 1581, painted shortly before the Fenton voyage, Banister is shown conducting an anatomy at the Barber-Surgeons' Hall.[116] This was for purposes of instruction. Statute made the bodies of executed criminals available for the purpose. The hall was in Monkwell Street, which abutted Silver Street, and it was still there when Shakespeare became a local resident.

Banister probably died in 1610, and was buried at Saint Olave's Church in Silver Street. His epitaph there is long gone (the church was destroyed in the Great Fire of 1666); but D'Arcey Power, the eminent surgeon and writer, has left us the full text of it – without, unfortunately, stating where he got it from.[117]

Banister's residence in Silver Street, coupled with his death in 1610, would make him a likely acquaintance of Shakespeare, and thus able to give Shakespeare an account of the Fenton voyage. There are, however, some who doubt that Banister died in 1610; although, as D'Arcey Power had details of Banister's epitaph, it is difficult to see how he might have been mistaken as to the date of his death. But the *Oxford Dictionary of National Biography* puts Banister's death (albeit with a question mark) in 1599 and Charles Nicholl, writer of *The Lodger*, the best account by far of Shakespeare's time in Silver Street, prefers 1599. Nicholl states that Banister 'was not co-resident' there with Shakespeare.[118]

We need not be too concerned, however, with the question mark over when Banister died because there is some certainty about the last years of Lewis Otmore, the other surgeon on the voyage. He served as Warden of the Barber-Surgeons in 1596 and 1601[119] and was buried in 1605 at the church of Saint Lawrence Jewry, a short walk from Silver Street. Shakespeare had every opportunity to meet and talk with him.

However Shakespeare came across Fenton's plan to plant a colony in Saint Helena and become its king, it is reasonable to conclude that he turned to this unique event when writing *The Tempest*. If there are any rivals for this they have yet to be put forward in any study of his sources. Coupled with Dom Fernando as the prototype Caliban, we have, I believe, found Shakespeare's island.

X
Epilogue

The Tempest ends with the actor who has played the part of Prospero returning to the stage (or simply being left there alone by the rest of the cast) to deliver a fairly standard plea for applause:

> With the help of your good hands.
> Gentle breath of yours my sails
> Must fill, or else my project fails,
> Which was to please.
>
> (Epilogue, 12–13)

The author of a book does not seek applause but is equally hopeful that he will have provided both entertainment and some food for thought to the reader.

As a lawyer, I am used to presenting a case and leaving it to others to judge whether it succeeds. The case for Saint Helena being the island of *The Tempest* relies primarily on two things: the identification of Dom Fernando as the model for Caliban and Edward Fenton's plan to colonize the island and become its king. Each of these is, I believe, convincing in its own right as providing a source for the play. Taken together, each of them provides corroboration of the other. We may accept one as a coincidence, but two must establish a case.

Postscript
Ban', Ban', Ca-Caliban

Shakespeare often used stock names for his characters, sometimes in more than one play: Antonio, for example (Prospero's usurping brother in *The Tempest*), is the name most used by Shakespeare in his plays. (More famously, it is also the name of the title character in *The Merchant of Venice*.) But he also invented names, usually to tell us something about the character he was introducing. Miranda's name exemplifies this. It is derived from the Latin verb *miror*, 'to wonder'. In Italian, it becomes the adjective *mirando*, which means 'wondrous'. When, in the second scene of *The Tempest*, Ferdinand meets Miranda, we have the lines:

> FERDINAND   My prime request,
> I do last pronounce, is (O, you wonder!)
> If you be maid or no?
>
> MIRANDA   No wonder, sir,
> But certainly a maid.
>
> (1.2.426–429)

At this point, she has not told him her name; she keeps it back until 3.1.36. The point, of course, is that Ferdinand had instantly, at their first meeting, seen her as the personification of her name.

Shakespeare certainly coined Caliban's name, and there is general agreement among scholars that the name was intended to tell us something about Caliban; but nobody has ever been able to show with any certainty what this might be. If there is a clue, we should be able to find it in the play – but we will first look at the competing theories.

Caliban is an anagram of can(n)ibal. Whether Shakespeare intended it to be taken as such is a different matter. 'I am a weakish speller' is an anagram of William Shakespeare, but nobody has ever argued that this is how he came by his name. Nevertheless, the anagram theory has wide acceptance. The problem with the theory is that spelling was erratic in the late sixteenth and early seventeenth centuries (as we have seen from contemporary documents quoted in this book, wherever I have left the original spelling unchanged), and the anagram was not much used as a device. Standardized spelling came much later. It was the need for a comprehensive and authoritative dictionary that caused a group of London booksellers to commission Samuel Johnson to compile one in the eighteenth century. The now famous work took Johnson nine years to complete; his *A Dictionary of the English Language* appeared in 1755. It is ironic that it was Johnson – having provided the perfect vehicle for the standardization of English spelling – who then became the first person to put forward (in print, at least) the suggestion that Shakespeare used the device of an anagram to arrive at Caliban's name, an idea that he credited to Richard Farmer, of Emmanuel College, Cambridge.[120]

A playwright who indulged himself in anagrams in the early Jacobean period would have done so at substantial risk of no one recognizing them as such. In 1892, H. H. Furness, the editor of the first Arden edition of the play, questioned whether it was likely:

> ...that when *The Tempest* was acted before the motley audience of the Globe Theatre, there was a single auditor who, on hearing Prospero speak of Caliban, bethought him of the Caribbean Sea, and instantly surmised that his name was a metathesis of Cannibal? Under this impression, the appearance of the monster without a trace of his bloodthirsty characteristic must have been disappointing.[121]

Even if one treats the assonance between 'cannibal' and 'Caliban' as an audible play on these words (an audience listens, it does not read the script) there is a second difficulty, which Furness identifies: Caliban may have had a number of unsavoury habits, but eating people does not seem to have been one of them. Shakespeare referred to cannibals several times in his plays, and his usage of the word is clear. In *Henry VI, part 3*; *Othello*; and *Coriolanus* – all written by Shakespeare before he penned *The Tempest* – he expects his audience to know and appreciate that the principal requirement for a cannibal is an appetite for human flesh, as in: 'He had been cannibally given, he might have boiled and eaten him too.' (*Coriolanus* 5.5.188–189.)

The anagram theory is frequently treated by commentators on the play as an established fact, but continued acceptance of it is based on little more than constant repetition of the idea. As the Chinese proverb puts it, it takes only three men to make a tiger.

There have, however, been other suggestions as to the derivation of Caliban's name. Alden T. Vaughan and Virginia Mason Vaughan have set these out in their *Shakespeare's Caliban: A Cultural History*. These range over *kalebon*, an Arabic word for 'vile dog'; the Hindu *Kalee-ban* (a 'satyr of Kalee, the Hindu Proserpine'); the German word for a codfish (*kabliau*); and more. The only theory (other than the anagram one) that the Vaughans treat as likely to have provided Shakespeare with a prompt is that Caliban's name came from the distinctly similar sounding *cauliban*, a Romany word for 'blackness'. The Romany language had been known in England for a hundred years or so prior to Shakespeare writing *The Tempest*, but there can have been few in Shakespeare's audience who spoke or understood it. It is not a convincing derivation.

Shakespeare frequently combined two words to form a single name. Sycorax, the name of Caliban's mother, is an example of this. A look at how her name was constructed is of interest, as the same process of building a name may explain how Caliban came by his. Sycorax seems to be a composite word, incorporating 'corax', meaning a member of the crow family of birds, which includes the raven, *Corvus corax*. There is some support for this in the text, when Caliban enters on stage for the first time:

> As wicked dew as ere my mother brushed
> With raven's feather from unwholesome fen
> Drop on you both.
>   (1.2.321–323)

The origin of the first part of Sycorax's name has proved more elusive. In the case of Caliban, however, I suggest that we can trace both parts – his name, like Sycorax's, appearing to have been constructed from two components.

There is a scene in *The Tempest* where Caliban gets drunk, and, in a piece of doggerel, he divides his name into two parts:

> No more dams I'll make for fish,
> Nor fetch in firing at requiring,
> Nor scrape trenchering, nor wash dish.
> Ban' ban' Ca-caliban,
> Has a new master, get a new man.
>
> (2.2.176–180)

These lines have not attracted much attention from the various editors of editions of the play, who generally suggest that they simply show Caliban to be intoxicated; which the audience will have realized by this time anyway.

What the lines actually demonstrate is Shakespeare detaching the last three letters of Caliban's name, and emphasizing this by repetition; he is deconstructing it for us. It draws the attention of the audience to 'ban'. The meaning of 'ban' was clear in Shakespeare's time: to utter curses.[122]

One of Caliban's most famous lines is:

> You taught me language, and my profit on't
> Is I know how to curse.
>
> (1.2.364–365)

And curse Caliban does throughout the play. Shakespeare's audience would have recognized this element in Caliban's name and quickly seen its aptness.

Caliban's 'Ban' ban' Ca-caliban' gives an opportunity for some cursing – and a touch of bawdiness as well. Although lost on audiences today, just about every person present and listening to this in Shakespeare's time would have recognized 'caca' as an obscenity. *Cacafuego* was the nickname of the Spanish galleon *Nuestra Senora de la Conception*, captured by Drake off the Pacific coast of South America in 1579 during his epic circumnavigation. The treasure taken from it was of immense value, and it made Drake both rich and famous. The name *Cacafuego* was well known in Elizabethan and early Jacobean England. The second part of it clearly means 'fire' – as in Tierra del Fuego ('land of fire'). Taken as a whole, *Cacafuego* translates – and Shakespeare's audience would have readily appreciated this – as 'shitfire'. Caliban's rhyme would have raised plenty of laughter at the Globe.

But, as with Sycorax, it is more difficult to pin down where the first part of Caliban's name originated. We have already looked at Pigafetta's account of the first circumnavigation and must now revisit it. As we have seen, it contains references to Sycorax's Patagonian god Setebos, including in a glossary of *Words of the Pathagonian Giants*.[123] The glossary gives us ninety words, rendered phonetically, together with their meanings. These include: 'The great devil *Setebos*', 'The old man *Calischen*', and 'The young man *Callemi*'. Nobody reading this would have been left in much doubt as to what the prefix for 'man' was in the language of the

Tehuelche people. If also aware of the name of an Inuit captive – Calichough[124] – brought back to England by Frobisher in 1577, the reader might even have thought the prefix universal in the Americas. I believe that Shakespeare simply intended Caliban's name to convey 'cursing man' – which is what he is in the play.

Bibliography

Ackroyd, Peter 2005. *Shakespeare: The Biography*. London: Chatto and Windus.

Barbour, Richmond. 2009. *The Third Voyage Journals: Writing and Performance in the London East India Company, 1607–10*. New York: Palgrave Macmillan.

Bate, Jonathan. 1997. *The Genius of Shakespeare*. London: Picador.

Beeching, Jack, ed. 1972, *Hakluyt: Voyages and Discoveries*. London: Penguin Books.

Blackburn, Julia. 1991. *The Emperor's Last Island: A Journey to St Helena*. London: Secker and Warburg.

Blench, J. W. 1964. *Preaching in England in the late Fifteenth and Sixteenth Centuries*. Oxford: Basil Blackwell.

Bryson, Bill. 2007. *Shakespeare*. London: Harper Press.

Butterworth, Hezekiah. 1899. *The Story of Magellan: And the Discovery of the Philippines*. New York: D. Appleton and Company.

Cannan, Edward. 1992. *Churches of the South Atlantic Islands 1502—1991*. Oswestry: Anthony Nelson.

Carey, Daniel and Claire Jowitt, eds. 2012. *Richard Hakluyt and Travel Writing in Early Modern Europe*. Farnham: Ashgate Publishing (for the Hakluyt Society).

Crane, Nicholas. 2002 *Mercator: The Man Who Mapped the Planet*. New York: Henry Holt and Company.

Dakin, Nicholas. 2011 *John Dee of Mortlake*. London: Barnes and Mortlake History Society.

Donaldson, Ian. 2011. *Ben Jonson: A Life*. Oxford: Oxford University Press.

Donno, Elizabeth Story. 1976. *An Elizabethan in 1582*. London: The Hakluyt Society.

Fogg, Nicholas. 2013. *Hidden Shakespeare*. Stroud: Amberley Publishing.

Foster, Sir William. 1940, *The Voyages of Sir James Lancaster to Brazil and the East Indies 1591–1603*. London: The Hakluyt Society.

Gosse, Philip. 1990. *St Helena 1502–1938*. Oswestry: Anthony Nelson.

Halliwell, James Orchard. 1841–1842. *The Private Diary of Dr. John Dee*. London: The Camden Society.

Hancox, Joy. 2001. *Kingdom for a Stage: Magicians and Aristocrats in the Elizabethan Theatre*. Stroud: Sutton Publishing.

Harrison, G. B. *Menaphon and A Margarite of America*. 1927. Oxford: Basil Blackwell.

Keay, John. *The Honourable Company: A History of the English East India Company*. 1991. Harper Collins: London.

Kermode, Frank. 2004. *The Age of Shakespeare*. London: Weidenfeld and Nicolson.

Kipling, Rudyard. 2 July, 1898. 'How Shakspere Came to Write the 'Tempest.' Letter to *The Spectator*. Re-published 1916. New York: Dramatic Museum of Columbia University.

Massinger, Philip. 2010. *The Renegado*. Edited by Michael Neill. London: Methuen Drama.

McDermott, James. 2001. *Martin Frobisher, Elizabethan Privateer*. New Haven and London: Yale University Press.

Nicholl, Charles. 2007. *The Lodger: Shakespeare on Silver Street*. London: Allen Lane.

Parry, Glyn. 2011. *The Arch-Conjuror of England*. New Haven and London: Yale University Press.

Pigafetta, Antonio. 1975. *Magellan's Voyage: A Narrative Account of the First Circumnavigation*, translated and edited by R. A. Skelton. London: The Folio Society.

Quinn, David Beers. 1975. *The Last Voyage of Thomas Cavendish 1591—1592*. Chicago: University of Chicago Press.

Ridley, Jasper. 1998. *A Brief History of the Tudor Age*. London: Constable and Co.

Lee, Sidney, Sir, C. T. Onions, C. T., and Charles Talbut. 1916. *Shakespeare's England*. Oxford: Clarendon Press.

Southworth, John. 2002., *Shakespeare the Player*. Stroud: Sutton Publishing.

Taylor, E. G. R. 1963. *A Regiment for the Sea*. Cambridge: The Hakluyt Society.

———. 1959. *The Troublesome Voyage of Captain Edward Fenton 1582–1583*. The Hakluyt Society. Cambridge: Cambridge University Press.

Taylor, Gary. 1990. *Reinventing Shakespeare*. London: The Hogarth Press.

Vaughan, Alden T. and Virginia Mason Vaughan. 1991. *Shakespeare's Caliban: A Cultural History*. Cambridge University Press.

———. 1999. *The Tempest*, edited by Alden T. Vaughan and Virginia Mason Vaughan. Walton-on-Thames: Thomas Nelson and Sons Ltd.

Wells, Stanley. 2007. *Shakespeare and Co*. London: Penguin Books.

Wilson, Ian. 1993. *Shakespeare: The Evidence.* London: Headline Book Publishing.

Woollet, Benjamin. 2001. *The Queen's Conjuror: The Life and Magic of Dr Dee.* London: Harper Collins.

Young, Sidney. 1890. *The Annals of the Barber-Surgeons of London.* London: Blades, East & Blades.

Notes

Introduction

1. *The Telegraph*, 27 January 2012.

2. Frey, *The Tempest and the New World*, 38, 34; cited by Alden T. Vaughan and Virginia Mason Vaughan in *Shakespeare's Caliban*. I have adopted the Vaughans' reversal of Frey's statements; which, as they say, does not distort Frey's meaning.

I Here Is Everything Advantageous to Life

3. Cannan, 24.

4. Ibid.

5. *Hakluyt's Collection of the Early Voyages, Travels and Discoveries of the English Nation*, Vol. II, London, 1810, 415.

6. Barret states: 'the ships which come from India come again [i.e. on the return voyage to Portugal] but slenderly victualled, because there groweth no corn there, neither make they any wine: but the ships which come from Portugal to the Indies touch not in the said island, because they set out being sufficiently furnished with bread and water from Portugal for eight months' voyage'.

7. Cannan, 23.

8. Skilfully.

9. Clear.

10. A unit of length of 200 yards (600 feet/183m). In fact, the fall drops 295 feet (90m).

11. I have abridged this and used modern spelling.

12. The Cape of Good Hope.

13. I have again abridged this and used modern spelling. 'Nova Hispania' is Mexico and the 'Cape of Bona Speranza' is the Cape of Good Hope.

14. Linschoten, 173. I have abridged this and used modern spelling.

15. Foster, 16.

16. Ibid., 28–29.

17. Edmond Malone, ed. *The Plays and Poems of William Shakespeare*, London, 1821, Vol. XV, 13.

18. Referred to in some sources as the *Red Dragon*.

19. Foster, 116–117.

20. 1.1.28.

21. Foster, 118.

22. Ibid.

23. Violent waves; but also, of a person, meaning unruly: *The Tempest*, ed. Vaughan and Vaughan, ed., 145, n. 17.

24. 1.1.116/117.

25. Cited in Barbour, 244. Barbour states that these entries 'initially surfaced in the *European Magazine* [December 1825] as the afterthought to an article by one Ambrose Gunthio on *Hamlet*'s lately rediscovered First Quarto.' I have modernized the spelling.

26. Barbour, 27.

27. Edward Haie in Hakluyt, *Principal Navigations*, 8:47; cited in Barbour, 260 (n. 72).

28. Harrison, 111. The extract is taken from Lodge's dedicatory address.

29. Ibid., 223.

30. Ibid., 120–122.

31. Quinn, 122.

32. Ibid., 124.

33. Diana's Peak.

34. *Dictionary of National Biography* (1908 reissue), Vol. III, 1271–1272. The attribution to Jane reads: 'The last Voyage of the worshipfull M. Thomas Candish *(sic)*, esquire, intended for the South Sea, the Philippines, and the coast of China, with three tall ships and two barks. Written by M. J. Jane' Hakluyt, 1589, vol. iii.'

35. See also Treasure and Dawson, 224.

36. Foster, 119.

37. Quinn, 126.

38. Ibid., 132.

39. John Chamberlain, cited by Wilson, 285.

II The Tempest

40. The much-cited Revels Accounts for that year.

41. *To the memory of My Beloved the Author, Mr. William Shakespeare*: Jonson's contribution to the First Folio of 1623.

42. Mahood, 168.

43. Beeching suggests, for example (24), that 'a more meticulous scrutiny' of Hakluyt's work might enable the date of composition of *Twelfth Night* to be established more precisely.

44. Ibid., 27.

45. *The voyage out of London of M. Iohn Eldred to Trypolis in Syria by sea, and from thence by land and river to Babylon and Balsara. 1585.* Eldred wrote: 'I departed out of London in the ship called the Tiger.' He later noted the death in Aleppo of William Barret, whose account of the discovery of Saint Helena I have referred to in chapter 1. Barret's account immediately follows Eldred's in Hakluyt, making it likely that Shakespeare read both.

46. Still then used by child actors – the Children of the Chapel Royal – the King's Men took it over in 1608.

47. An extensive extract from Strachey's letter is set out at Appendix 1, 288–302 of Vaughan and Vaughan, *The Tempest*.

48. G. A. Wilkes, 7.

49. J. D. Rogers, *Voyages and Exploration: Geography: Maps: Shakespeare's England*, Vol. 1, 170.

III The Great Globe Itself

50. 2.1.5.

51. 2.1.6.

52. Butterworth, 13.

53. *The Tempest*, ed. Vaughan, p. 237, n. 48. The note states: 'Given the difficulties of travel in that period, the odds were in favour of the broker.'

54. If Shakespeare needed help with the version in Italian, he could have turned to John Florio. Florio, tutor in Italian to Queen Anne (the wife of James I), is considered to have been an associate of Shakespeare. Florio was no stranger to translating travel narratives. As early as 1580, he had translated Jacques Cartier's narratives for Hakluyt (Carey and Jowitt, 49–50). Certainly, Shakespeare had no difficulty in working from texts in Italian: the plots of *Othello* and *The Merchant of Venice* were substantially derived from Italian sources not yet translated into English. Shakespeare is likely to have had a good grasp of French (or assistance with it if not), since he lived in a French-speaking household from around 1603 to 1605. His residence in Silver Street, London, is well covered in *The Lodger*, by Charles Nicholl.

55. Skelton, 6.

56. Ibid., 34–35.

57. Ibid., 42.

58. Ibid., 48.

59. Ibid., 42.

60. Ibid., 45.

IV We Must Prepare to Meet with Caliban

61. *The Tempest*, ed. Kermode.

62. It was compiled by two of Shakespeare's fellow actors, John Heminge and Henry Condell, and published under the title *Mr. William Shakespeares Comedies, Histories, & Tragedies.*

63. The 'Names of the Actors'.

64. Ibid.

65. Ibid.

66. *The Tempest*, ed. Luce, xxxv.

67. Vaughan, *Shakespeare's Caliban*, 43.

V This Island's Mine

68. Philip Massinger, *The Renegado*, ed. Michael Neill, 235. The meaning of 'renegade' at that time was: 'A person who abandons one religious faith for another, esp. a Christian who becomes Muslim', *The New Shorter Oxford English Dictionary*.

69. Blackburn, chapter III. Blackburn clearly recognises Dom Fernando as a Caliban-type figure; the chapter

commences with a quote from Caliban in *The Tempest* – the opening lines of his speech commencing at 3.2.135.

70. Gosse, 6.

71. Ibid., 8.

72. Ibid., 9.

VI As You from Crimes Will Pardoned Be

73. Ibid., 10.

VII Rapt in Secret Studies

74. *The Alchemist*, II.vi.19–24. Taken from *Ben Jonson: Five Plays*, ed. G. A. Wilkes, 407.

75. Donaldson, 132.

76. By the scholar Meric Casaubon.

77. This has been much quoted, including by E. K. Chambers, *William Shakespeare*, vol. II, 326.

78. Halliwell, 26.

79. All entries in the diary are taken from Halliwell.

80. E. G. R. Taylor, 314.

81. The part of this work dealing with John Dee is fully set out in *John Dee of Mortlake*, by Nicholas Dakin, published by the Barnes and Mortlake History Society; from which I have taken the various extracts that follow in the text.

82. Dakin, 86.

83. www.british-history.ac.uk/london-environs/vol1/pp364-388; originally published by T. Cadell and W. Davies, London, 1792.

84. E. G. R. Taylor, Bibliography, xxi.

VIII When It Is Bak'd with Frost

85. Donno, *An Elizabethan in 1582*, 44.

86. McDermott, 106. The words are those of George Best, a 'gentleman-soldier' who sailed with Frobisher in the 1577 and 1578 voyages.

87. Today known as Kodlurnan Island.

88. McDermott, 211.

89. *A True Report of the Third and Last Voyage into Meta Incognita* (London, 1578).

90. Charles Francis Hall, an American, was the next non-Inuit visitor, during his 1860–1863 expedition.

91. Ellis, *A True Report*.

IX Had I Plantation of this Isle

92. Donno, *An Elizabethan in 1582*, 3.

93. 2.2.336–342.

94. J. W. Blench, 172, where it is referred to as *A learned and godly sermon, especially for all marryners* (London, 1581).

95. Ibid., 172.

96. Ibid., 173.

97. Diary entry for 15 February 1582, Donno, 85.

98. Beeching, 232.

99. This account is taken from Donno, 73–74.

100. Donno, *An Elizabethan in 1582*, 84 (n. 6).

101. Ibid., 88.

102. Ibid., 195–196.

103. The 'Names of the Actors'.

104. Vaughan and Vaughan, *Shakespeare's Caliban*, 41.

105. The *Prologue* to *The Arte of Rhetorique*, added in 1567, contains the following: '[I]f others never gette more by books than I have doen: it were better be a Carter, than a Scholer, for worldly profite.'

106. Taylor, 181–182.

107. *Narrative of William Hawkins 6 July 1583*; Taylor, *The Troublesome Voyage of Captain Edward Fenton*, 278. I have abridged this and modernized the spelling in part.

108. Ibid., 259.

109. Ibid., 262.

110. Ibid., 259.

111. Donno, *An Elizabethan in 1582*, 182.

112. Both Percy and Jeffery make it clear in their accounts that the need for wine was an issue, requiring a trip back to the Cape Verde Islands before proceeding to Saint Helena; see Taylor at 259 and 262.

113. 2.2.36–40.

114. 2.1.169.

115. 3.6.34–35

116. Now owned by Glasgow University; *Glasgow U.L., Hunter MS 364.*

117. Cited in Donno, *An Elizabethan in 1582*, 45. Donno states that the epitaph is quoted in D'Arcey Power, 'Notes on Early Portraits', 24–25.

118. Nicholl, 61.

119. Young, 7.

Postscript: Ban', Ban', Ca-Caliban

120. *The Plays of William Shakespeare*, ed. Samuel Johnson and George Stevens, Second Edition, Vol. I, p. 32, London, 1778.

121. *The Tempest*, ed. Furness, 5 (n. 10); cited in Vaughan, *Shakespeare's Caliban*, 31.

122. *The New Shorter Oxford English Dictionary*; the dictionary records the usage as now archaic.

123. Skelton, 54–55.

124. McDermott, 191.

Printed in Great Britain
by Amazon.co.uk, Ltd.,
Marston Gate.